THE BATTLE FOR THE JEWISH STATE

THE BATTLE FOR THE JEWISH STATE: HOW ISRAEL —AND AMERICA— CAN WIN

VICTORIA COATES

Foreword by
SENATOR TED CRUZ

BOOKS

NEW YORK • LONDON

First American edition published in 2024 by Encounter Books,
an activity of Encounter for Culture and Education, Inc.,
a nonprofit, tax-exempt corporation.
Encounter Books website address: www.encounterbooks.com

Manufactured in the United States and printed on
acid-free paper. The paper used in this publication meets
the minimum requirements of ANSI/NISO Z39.48-1992
(R 1997) (Permanence of Paper).

FIRST AMERICAN EDITION

LIBRARY OF CONGRESS CATALOGING-IN-PUBLICATION DATA
Library of Congress CIP data is available online under the following
ISBN 978-1-64177-455-0 and LCCN 2024045542

For my grandfather,
U.S. ARMY CAPTAIN HOWARD ALLEN DOWNEY,
who stormed up Utah Beach in the D-Day invasion
to liberate Europe from the Third Reich,
and for my mother,
ANNE DOWNEY GARDNER,
whose namesake anti-aircraft gun, the "BABY ANNE,"
was hunting Nazis when she was six months old.

CONTENTS

FOREWORD

The Rot Exposed:
Why the War on Israel is a War on America

THE HORRIFIC OCTOBER 7 terrorist attacks were the worst one-day massacre of Jews since the Holocaust. Hamas massacred, tortured, burned alive, raped, and kidnapped thousands of Israelis as part of an explicit genocidal war, which is ultimately being waged by the Ayatollah in Iran with help from antisemites around the world.

One of the lessons of that horrific day is the plain fact that Hamas's terrorist attacks and campaign are not targeting only Israel, nor are their victims confined only to the Middle East. This war is not just being waged against the United States, our citizens, and our national security interests. The objective of Israel's enemies is not just the elimination of the Jewish state, but also Western civilization, led by America, writ large.

In the hours and days after the October 7 attacks, Israel committed to utterly eradicating Hamas. That mission is one which should have drawn immediate, unequivocal, and material support from every part of the United States and the West. Instead, we saw opposition to Israel and support for Hamas from parts of the American political Left, including far too many elected officials, and outright antisemitic violence across America's college campuses. If there is any silver lining to the horror of October 7 it is that it exposed the extent of this rot—and it is critical to note, the crisis was exposed, not generated, on that day.

Victoria Coates has written an invaluable book on exactly this crisis, and the challenges and threats it poses not just to the existence of Israel but to the United States. In the pages that follow, Victoria lays bare the truth that so many have ignored or denied for too long: the war on Israel is not a distant conflict but a direct attack on America's interests, and indeed on our way of life. Defending Israel is not only a matter of supporting a key ally, although it most certainly is. Challenging hatred of Jews and the Jewish state is not just a vital task for our domestic political life, although it most certainly is. The challenge is far more direct and dire. The enemies of Israel are the enemies of America, they are on the march, and their hatred—and their goals—know no bounds or borders.

The situation has been in many ways in the making since the foundation of modern Israel in 1948 and has intensified since Israel's victory in the 1973 Yom Kippur War, after which the U.S.-Israel alliance was cemented. At the same time opposition to Israel coalesced across America's elite universities, which took up the cause of Palestinian terrorists, and in diplomatic circles in European capitals and Washington, D.C., where a fiction developed that it was somehow in America's interest to show balance between those terrorists and our Israeli allies.

Hamas's attack on October 7 should have forever ended any confusion about which side the United States must support—and support unequivocally. Hamas, alongside many other Palestinian groups, has long been considered a terrorist organization by the United States. Dozens of Americans were among those whom the terrorists raped, kidnapped, and killed. The tactics used by Hamas—including and especially the use of civilian human shields before, during, and after the attack—are ones that the United States has not only long condemned but has legislated against in a bipartisan fashion. In the years prior to October 7, I drafted and passed into law bipartisan legislation imposing mandatory sanctions on Hamas for the use of human shields, and unanimously passed a resolution condemning them for doing so. The issue used to be one that Republicans and Democrats could agree upon: Hamas seeks to destroy Israel and undermine the United States, they know they cannot defeat Israel militarily so they create Palestinian civilian casualties to generate international outrage against Israel by using human shields, and this tactic is an instance of using evil means to achieve an evil end.

It is worth noting that my mandatory sanctions were simply not enforced by the Biden-Harris administration. In retrospect evidence has been building up in recent years of a dangerous backsliding in support for—and clarity about—what is at stake in the war being waged against Israel, in Washington, D.C. and beyond. While hardly a secret, these developments are not well understood and have never been thoroughly documented.

The Battle for the Jewish State: How Israel—and America—Can Win provides immeasurably valuable insight to clarify the sources and motives of what we have witnessed since October 7, many of which are indeed entangled in antisemitism. The good news is that polling consistently documents support for Israel among a robust majority of Americans. The bad news is that that majority declines dramatically among younger Americans being educated in increasingly radicalized colleges and universities.

The antisemitism in American academia was publicly exposed on December 5, just two months after the Hamas attack. The Presidents of Harvard, MIT, and the University of Pennsylvania were called to testify before the House of Representatives' Committee for Education and the Work Force. The House was controlled by Republicans, who were committed to investigating the antisemitic violence that was sweeping campuses and endangering American Jewish students, and which had erupted visibly right after October 7. In the Senate, Leader Chuck Schumer studiously sought to shield the progressive wing of the Democrat Party from having to discuss let alone vote on what was happening.

In the pages that follow, Victoria shows the breadth, depth, and importantly sources and persistence of that violence—and what it means for America's future and security. The public record continues to be deliberately obfuscated. At that very hearing, the three witnesses had been carefully coached to hide the facts. They all used the same awkward, stilted legalese designed to obfuscate instead of clarify. Liz McGill of Penn, whose campus had witnessed significant outbreaks of antisemitism before October 7, refused to say that calling for the genocide of Jews would violate the university's code of conduct. MIT's Sally Kornbluth, when asked about chants for intifada, said they could only be considered genocidal against Jews "depending on the context." Claudine Gay of Harvard used the same phrase to equivocate on whether or not genocidal statements about Jews violated her university's code of conduct.

All three were egregious, but Gay's performance was particularly painful for me as an alumnus of the Harvard Law School. So many Harvard alums were appalled by what had been revealed as permitted, and even celebrated, in Cambridge after October 7. The questioning in the House hearing was led by one of them, Congresswoman Elise Stefanik (R-NY), and in the days after she and I wrote a letter to President Gay regarding her craven testimony:

> It is sickening that students at Harvard University are so steeped in their hatred for Israel that they have chosen to ignore reality, cheer on ruthless terrorists, and blame innocent civilians. This heinous statement and the support it received from over thirty student organizations across Harvard University should raise immediate concerns into Harvard's curriculum regarding the State of Israel. This type of unified hate and ignorance cannot be allowed at Harvard University, and you must investigate its origins.

I was honored to know the Holocaust survivor and human rights champion Elie Wiesel, and his memory, although always a blessing, has troubled me in the months since October 7. At the time of his death in 2016, I wrote:

> Elie Wiesel was a living testimony to the vow "Never Forget." Although he endured the unspeakable darkness of Auschwitz and Buchenwald, his defiant light burned ever brighter as he dedicated his talents to providing a voice not only for the Jewish victims of the Holocaust but also for the voiceless, the condemned, and the forsaken around the globe. Elie tirelessly reminded the

world that the savage horror of the Third Reich was not an aberration in the past that was defeated in World War II. He knew the potential for such genocidal evil remains with us in the present—and warned we must always be on our guard against it.

But what has been exposed since October 7 shows we are failing. Now no longer do we have the excuse of ignorance, and eradicating American antisemitism will be an integral component a larger civilizational battle that is now upon us.

The Battle for the Jewish State is a central part of the effort to arm Americans who support Israel and want and need to know what antisemitism is doing to us here at home. It is filled with the facts about the U.S.–Israel alliance and why it is critical to our own national security. Victoria was my National Security Advisor during my first five years in the Senate, for which I was immeasurably fortunate, and it was during that time that we laid the foundation for much of the work of which I'm proudest—including and especially my record on Israel and the Middle East more broadly.

Victoria's experience on these topics and in this region allows her to be a unique and invaluable voice on these issues. She was integral to the work done in the Trump administration to strengthen our alliance with Israel and across the Middle East, including moving our embassy to Jerusalem and inking the Abraham Accords—two successes which are inextricably linked. I was with Victoria in May 2018 when we opened our embassy in Jerusalem, as well as with her to celebrate at the White House in September 2020 for the joyful signing of the Abraham Accords.

I hope and pray we will be able to build on these successes going forward because while the best days of the U.S.–Israel alliance should be in front of us, that success is under constant threat by the progressive Left that rejects both Jews and the Jewish state. We will not be able to do so without Americans understanding the nature and the depth of what is at stake, which are meticulously documented in the subsequent pages of this book and ultimately rise to a ringing call to action.

The fight will be a long one. In July 2024, pro-Hamas antisemitic protesters flooded the streets of Washington to protest the visit of Israeli Prime Minister Benjamin Netanyahu. They made their way to Union Station, where they desecrated the Columbus monument, dragged down and burned three American flags, and replaced them with Palestinian flags. Americans were right to wonder how we got here.

I commend Victoria for her work and dedication to this cause. Together, we can and must ensure that the alliance between the United States and Israel remains unshakable, and that we remain ever vigilant against the forces that seek to tear us apart. Our future depends on it.

— SENATOR TED CRUZ

INTRODUCTION

THE FOUR CHAPTERS of *The Battle for the Jewish State: How Israel—and America—Can Win* attempt to answer some key questions and explain, in the wake of the October 7, 2023 Hamas attack on Israel, where we came from, where we are, and what our choices are going forward in terms of the U.S.–Israel alliance. My inescapable conclusion is that we are in a war for the survival of both Israel and America as we know them, and that it must be decisively won for not just our sakes, but for the sake of the rest of the world that still values what our countries represent: personal freedom, sovereignty, and opportunity.

This book is not a comprehensive history of Israel or of the peace process. It is an American perspective on why recent events in the Middle East in general and Israel in particular are critical to U.S. national security and what we might do about it. In the weeks—and now months—since October 7, I found myself fielding very similar queries from a range of sources such as fellow policymakers, journalists, foreign interlocutors, and interested friends, and imagined many Americans might be wondering the same things. They fell into four main categories.

After the immediate shock wore off and the aftermath of the attack took shape, the most frequent question was a befuddled "How did we get here?" The reflexive response of horror to the events of October 7, which even included the Biden administration for the most part, gave way in record time to equivocating attempts to justify the Palestinians' actions in Israel and to gross demonstrations of antisemitism in the United States. For most, this was a bizarre outcome. But, as perspective grew, it emerged as part of a concerted plan of war in which October 7 was only the first battle in a wider movement that also targets the United States.

The public-relations campaign against Israel intensified as the Gaza war dragged on, and President Biden's support for Israel flagged, leading many to ask, "Why is Israel the partner of choice for the United States in the Middle East?" Over the course of my life, as the nation of Israel has gone from being twenty to seventy-six years old, the answer to that question has evolved significantly. The relationship itself has changed under different presidents and prime ministers, and the question needs to be answered from a practical, American perspective, not by way of an abstract moral or religious rationale. In 2024, Israel is in fact the preeminent security and technology partner for the United States in the Middle East and increasingly integrated with our Arab partners, and that reality needs to be taken into account in any effective regional strategy.

Given all the support for the Palestinians that emerged in America on college campuses, not to mention in international organizations, after October 7, the next question became, "Is there an alternative to Israel in the Middle East if the Jewish state is so problematic?" The answer is yes, there are actually two options working in concert: the Palestinians and the Islamic Republic of Iran. There is now a long and undistinguished bipartisan history of failing attempts to make the Palestinians into the regional equivalent of the Israelis, and to insist that the two sides are on the same level from an American perspective. On Iran, while its regime has generally been considered a pariah for the decades after the 1979 revolution, first the Obama-Biden administration and now the Biden-Harris administration have tried to engage with it and degrade America's relationship with Israel in an attempt to reset the Middle East, with very little to show for the effort given Iran's resolutely hostile posture towards both the United States and Israel.

Finally, "What's next?" is a legitimate question to ask about the next twenty-five years of the U.S.–Israel relationship, as a year out from the October 7 attacks we appear to be at something of a crossroads. The 2024 election is a Reagan-style time for choosing in that the American people are for the first time confronted with two non-incumbents in the former president and sitting vice president, who nonetheless have well-established track records on Israel policy. This chapter traces their respective approaches and offers policy prescriptions designed to maximize the efficacy of the U.S.–Israel relationship as we approach its centenary in 2048.

Throughout the process of writing this book, I found myself haunted by the Zionist leader Ze'ev Jabotinsky's 1923 essay "The Iron Wall." Despite having been written more than two decades before the 1948 establishment of modern Israel, it contains two fundamental truths that are central to the crisis we confront today. First, until the Palestinians accept that the Jewish state is not going away, their "Plan A" will always be the eradication of the Jews. And second, to defend against the inevitable attacks, Israel must have impenetrable defenses, which increasingly come in the form of the alliance with the United States. Both these truths were demonstrated by the October 7 attacks and should guide our thinking going forward.

There is a concerted campaign that has been in the works since the 1970s to transform the history of both Israel and the United States away from the true story of two small, remote, and imperiled new countries, both based on a concept, that had no business thriving but which nonetheless became two of the most powerful countries in the world. These two Biblical Davids, if you will, are now portrayed as the equivalent of Goliaths—imperial and oppressive giants bent on death and destruction, a rhetorical process delineated by Joshua Muravchik in his 2015 book *Making David into Goliath* that is only accelerating today.

This Critical Race Theory–fueled attempt to revise history on a radical progressive model is informing a small but growing minority of Americans who see their own country, along with Israel, as the problem in the world. In fact, most Americans still believe that the best thing for the world is the preservation and promotion of the United States—and the Jewish state America has helped to establish. But as more and more young people are being taught that the opposite is true, it has become necessary to make the case for why the U.S.–Israel relationship is critical to American national security going forward, and why abandoning it would be a disaster not only for Israel but also for America. As old-fashioned as it may seem in 2024, this is a war and it needs to be won. That is why I wrote *The Battle for the Jewish State.*

ACKNOWLEDGMENTS

M ANY FRIENDS AND colleagues have contributed to *The Battle for the Jewish State* and any errors herein are mine and not theirs.

The last decade of visiting, watching, and thinking about Israel would not have happened if Senator Ted Cruz had not surprised me greatly by asking me to join his staff in 2013, and I am honored he agreed to write the foreword to this book. I made my first trip to the Holy Land with him the following year in the company of our then chief of staff, now Congressman, Chip Roy. Over the four years that followed, Senator Cruz's principled clarity and leadership on this issue resulted in concrete legislative victories supporting the U.S.–Israel alliance, from his cosponsorship of the Jerusalem Recognition Act to the bipartisan resolution condemning Hamas's use of human shields to the bill providing grounds for the refusal of visas for U.N. diplomats owing to their engagement in terrorism—all critical work he continues to this day. I owe a huge debt to the fellow Cruz staff members who supported this work, including my once and forever right-hand Samantha Leahy McLean, David Milstein, Paul Teller, and Omri Ceren.

Great thanks are also due to President Donald J. Trump, who gave me a front-row seat to the extraordinary achievements on Israel/Middle East policy of his first term. I served under all four of his National Security Advisors—Michael Flynn, H. R. McMaster, John Bolton, and Robert O'Brien—at the White House, and each gave me increasing opportunities to work on these issues. When I moved into the Middle East Directorate on the NSC, I was immensely fortunate to have my disaster twin, Robert Greenway, who has forgotten more about Iran than I will ever know, as my deputy and friend. My special #MENA family, I'm not going to name you, but you know who you are. Thank you for your service.

I benefitted greatly from my work with other Trump-administration colleagues, notably K. T. McFarland, Keith Kellogg, Charlie Kupperman, Mira Ricardel, Sarah Tinsley, Kevin Harrington, Fred Fleitz, Jared Kushner, Jason Greenblatt, David Friedman, John Rakolta, John Abizaid, Justin Silberman, Carla Sands, David Fisher, Aryeh Lightstone, Chris Miller, Jonathan "JW" White, Nadia Schadlow, Erin Walsh, Joel Rayburn, Bonnie Glick, Simone Ledeen, Mike Pompeo, Russ Vought, Brian McCormick, Mike Duffy, Robert Wilkie, Ellie Cohanim, Amanda Rothschild, Carrie Fillipetti, Sigal Mandelker, Marshall Billingslea, Morgan Ortagus, Len Khordokovsky, Brian Hook, Nathan Sales, Heather Nauert, Elliott Abrams, Tara Rigler, Mike Martin, and Cale Brown. Special thanks also to President Trump's Secretaries of Energy Rick Perry and Dan Brouillette, as well as Aliya Boyer and Landon Derentz, who made my time at DoE such a remarkable and educational experience.

I am very fortunate that Roger Kimball and his exceptional team at Encounter Books led by Sam Schneider, Elizabeth Bachmann, and Ben Riley were willing to jump into the pick-up game that was *The Battle for the Jewish State* to get it out at "warp speed." I am thrilled to now be an Encounter author twice over.

I am immensely grateful for the friendship and guidance of Ambassador Ronald Lauder and his team, including Allen Roth, David Goder, and especially Steven Schneier.

Over the last ten years I have built strong relationships with many Israelis who have contributed enormously to my understanding of the Jewish state, so thanks to Prime Minister Benjamin Netanyahu, Ron Dermer, Jordana Cutler, Meier Ben Shabbat, Reuven Azar, Alon Uschpiz, Zohar Palti, Dor Shapira, Benjy Krasna, Caroline Glick, Zeev Orenstein, and David Aaronson.

I am deeply fortunate in my current home at The Heritage Foundation and for the support from President Kevin Roberts, Executive Vice President Derrick Morgan, and for the editorial expertise of Tom Spence, without whom this book would not have been possible. Many others across the organization have also contributed, and my special thanks go out to Robert Greenway (again) and the rest of my fantastic team at the Kathryn and Shelby Cullom Davis Institute for National Security and Foreign Policy and all the Heritage members who support our work, first and foremost Diana Davis Spencer and Abby Spencer Moffat, who gave our Institute its proud name.

My dear friend Doug Feith is responsible for my introduction to Ze'ev Jabotinsky, whose thinking is central to the premise of this book.

Finally, last but never least my thanks to my ever loving and forgiving family, especially my mother and grandfather, to whom this book is dedicated, and as always to George, Gardner, and Gowen, who have gamely joined my improbable journey to the Holy Land and beyond.

ACRONYM LIST

AEDPA	Antiterrorism and Effective Death Penalty Act
AIPAC	American Israel Public Affairs Committee
AEW&C	Airborne Early Warning & Control
AWACS	Airborne Warning And Control System
BDS	Boycott, Divestiture, Sanctions
CRT	Critical Race Theory
DFLP	Democratic Front for the Liberation of Palestine
DNI	Director of National Intelligence
EMGF	Eastern Mediterranean Gas Forum
ESF	Economic Support Funds
FTA	Free Trade Agreement
FDI	Foreign Direct Investment
FTO	Foreign Terrorist Organization
GMO	Government Media Office
HLF	Holy Land Foundation
IAEA	International Atomic Energy Agency
ICC	International Criminal Court
ICJ	International Court of Justice
IDF	Israel Defense Forces
INARA	Iran Nuclear Agreement Review Act
IRGC	Islamic Revolutionary Guard Corps
ISIS	Islamic State in Iraq and Syria

JCPOA	Joint Comprehensive Plan Of Action
JPOA	Joint Plan Of Action
MESA	Middle East Strategic Alliance
MOU	Memorandum Of Understanding
NGO	Non-Governmental Organization
NSC	National Security Council
OCHA	United Nations Office for the Coordination of Humanitarian Affairs
P5	Permanent 5 Members of the U.N. Security Council *(United States, France China, Russia, United Kingdom)*
P5+1	P5 Members + Germany
PFLP	Popular Front for the Liberation of Palestine
PLF	Palestinian Liberation Front
PLO	Palestine Liberation Organization
PMD	Potential Military Dimension
PMF	Popular Mobilization Forces of Iraq
QME	Qualitative Military Edge
SDGT	Specially Designated Global Terrorist
SDI	Strategic Defense Initiative
SFFA	Students For Fair Admissions
UNHRC	United Nations Human Rights Commission
UNRWA	United Nations Relief Works Agency
UNSCR	United Nations Security Council Resolution
WCK	World Central Kitchen

CHAPTER ONE: OCTOBER 7 WAS ONLY THE BEGINNING

How did we get here?

MOST OF WORLD reacted with horror to Hamas's savage attacks against Israel on October 7, 2023. The atrocities, captured in footage shot by the terrorists themselves, were not the sanitized, remote violence of a video game but gut-wrenchingly real—women raped, babies impaled, men tortured and left to bleed out, survivors spirited away by their tormentors to a fresh hell of captivity. Scores of young revelers slaughtered at a music festival in southern Israel. And all this was followed by scenes of the terrorists and the people of Gaza celebrating together in an ecstatic delirium of death and revenge.

October 7 was the largest terrorist attack in the history of Israel, and the equivalent of thirteen 9/11s in the United States. Some 1,500 highly trained terrorists had swarmed into Israel in automobiles, on motorbikes, and on hang gliders to kill Jews. While its targets were primarily Israelis, Hamas didn't care that others—Asians, Africans, Europeans, and Latin Americans, not to mention dozens of Americans—were caught in the violence. The goal was not victory in a territorial sense, as a rational person might understand it. It was genocide—the eradication of Jews—plain and simple. The elite Hamas terrorists were followed by a wave of Palestinian Islamic Jihad fighters, then by Palestinian civilians (so-called), some of whom had been employed in Israel, who saw the holes in the security barrier around the Gaza Strip.

These Palestinians ostensibly had no warning of the attacks, but spontaneously and enthusiastically leapt into the fray. Armed with knives and axes, they joined the violent mayhem and raped and murdered alongside Hamas. They also looted anything they could find, from motorbikes to women's underwear, some making multiple trips for booty.

The Palestinians are not unsophisticated—they have smartphones, watch YouTube, and are beneficiaries of the largest single refugee effort in history, the United Nations Relief Works Agency (UNRWA), as well as a host of other international nongovernmental organizations (NGOs), to the tune of billions of dollars of international aid. Yet their default mechanism is sadistic savagery. The question is whether their predilection for violence, which even their supporters acknowledge, is sociopathic, or is rather a legitimate—even laudable—Palestinian tactic to achieve their goal of replacing the Jewish state with a Palestinian one, "from the river to the sea."

As the shock wore off, it appeared that October 7 was only the beginning of the most recent iteration of the war that has been going on for nearly a century between Israel and its Arab neighbors. Since the 1980s, however, Israel has not faced a direct military threat from an Arab nation, though its internal and external terrorist enemies have been supported by the Islamic Republic of Iran, which is responsible for 90 percent of Hamas's financing. It is no coincidence that Iran experienced a massive economic windfall from oil sales when President Biden stopped enforcing Trump-era sanctions in 2021, and its funding increased to the point that Hamas could launch an attack on the scale of October 7. It is also no coincidence that after months of President Biden's tepid and equivocating support of Israel, Iran was emboldened to take its long proxy war with the Jewish state out of the shadows and, on April 13, 2024, launch the largest single state-to-state direct missile and drone attack on Israel.[1]

Israel has decisively won each previous military engagement with the Palestinians and their supporters (including Iran), although, uniquely in history, no one has had the courage simply to tell the Palestinians that they lost, the war is over, and here are the terms. If they had, generations of Palestinian suffering might have been prevented, as might the anguish of October 7. Instead, the genocidal plotting went on until it burst into the open with this spectacularly gruesome attack. The resulting conflict, by arousing the antipathy of the American Left, has become a more serious threat to Israel than anything Hamas might do independently, making it all the more imperative that Israel—and by extension the United States—wins.

Springing the Trap

THE PALESTINIANS LIKE TO refer to the establishment of the modern state of Israel in 1948 as the "nakba," or disaster. They considered the presidency of Donald J. Trump a second nakba. While his term had begun with a congenial visit to the White House in May 2017 by the president of the Palestinian Authority, Mahmoud Abbas, which left Abbas "hopeful" about the prospects for a deal with Israel, things rapidly went downhill.[2] Unable or unwilling to control Palestinian unrest on the Temple Mount in Jerusalem that summer, Abbas eventually took the unprecedented step of cutting off the security cooperation with Israel that was critical for reducing violence in the West Bank after the Second Intifada, which raged from 2000–05. But by 2017, Abbas was ready to jettison that successful cooperation in order to retain his political control of the West Bank.

Then, in September of that year, Abbas traveled to New York to address the United Nations General Assembly and gave his boilerplate speech on Israel's culpability for Palestinian attacks on Jews and America's culpability for its support of Israel.[3] Complaining about colonial occupation and calling on the International Criminal Court (ICC) to prosecute Israeli officials, he said nothing he had not said before. But this time, there was a new member of the audience: President Trump.

During their White House meeting, Abbas had persuaded the president that he was a legitimate partner for peace and that the Israelis, especially Prime Minister Benjamin Netanyahu, refused to make a deal. But it was clear from his U.N. speech that Abbas was equally obstinate— if not more so. He also expressed no gratitude to the United States, as the single largest donor to the Palestinian-aid vehicles, namely UNRWA, for which Abbas demanded still more funding.

Previous American presidents had shrugged off such rhetoric as Palestinian grandstanding, but for President Trump it struck a nerve. Why should the American taxpayer be on the hook for people who were both unappreciative of American support and antisemitic? Abbas and his acolytes didn't even bother to hide it while they were on our own soil. The Trump administration undertook a thorough review of its Israel–Palestinian policy, concluding that it simply wasn't working. Critics denounced the subsequent decisions to end Palestinian funding and the announcement of the president's intention to move the U.S. embassy from Tel Aviv to Jerusalem,[4] predicting an unprecedented explosion of violence in the region.

Nothing of the sort took place. Despite incessant provocations from Iran during President Trump's term of office—particularly after he ceased compliance with the 2015 Joint Comprehensive Plan of Action (JCPOA), President Obama's misbegotten nuclear deal with Iran—the Israeli–American alliance entered a new era as the U.S. position was made crystal clear for the first time. No longer would the United States turn a blind eye to Palestinian incitements to violence and antisemitism, nor would America indulge in a moral equivalency between Israel and the Palestinians.

The world was on notice that Israel was a critical American ally. We would help the Palestinians if they were amenable to our terms but would no longer indulge the fantasy that their cause was equivalent in any way to America's alliance with Israel. In fact, in this worldview, resolution of the Israel–Palestinian conflict, while desirable, is not vital to U.S. national-security interests in the Middle East. Countering threats from Iran and the Muslim Brotherhood while integrating Israel as a point of American power projection into the region most definitely are.

With remarkable speed, much of the Middle East got on board with this program. After the U.S. embassy was moved in May 2018, the recognition of the Golan Heights as sovereign Israeli territory and important changes to the legal framework of Judea and Samaria drew little or no significant reaction. America stood firmly and unequivocally with Israel in international forums from the United Nations to the ICC in the understanding that their attacks on Israel were ultimately aimed at America itself.

The results of these new policies spoke for themselves. On September 15, 2020, President Trump hosted the signing of the historic Abraham Accords between Israel, the United Arab Emirates, and Bahrain at the White House, which were followed by an Israeli agreement with Morocco, and progress in negotiations with Sudan and Kosovo. These peace deals, the first between Israel and Muslim-majority countries in a quarter-century, were achieved because of President Trump's decision to abandon generations of failed policies designed to tempt the Palestinians into co-operation and depreciating the importance of its relationship with Israel to get a deal on the Palestinian issue. Unfortunately, President Trump's successor failed to understand this cause and effect. From day one, the Biden administration reaffirmed the moral equivalency between Israel and the Palestinians, which had bedeviled U.S. policy in the region for half a century. In the aftermath of October 7, we found out just how destructive that approach was, both abroad and at home.

Before the smoke of the terrorist attacks had cleared and while Israel was still collecting bodies and identifying who had been taken hostage by the terrorists, the pro-Hamas riots started. But they weren't in the Middle East, which beyond Israel was strikingly quiet. The Arab countries that had historically seized on such episodes to trumpet their commitment to the Palestinian cause and demonize Israel refrained from their standard rhetoric, issuing far more measured statements.[5] Friday sermons in mosques, traditionally incendiary, were tempered. The feared "Arab Street" was remarkable for its calm.

Not so in Europe and the United States. Paris, London, New York, and Los Angeles erupted in demonstrations that were overtly pro-Hamas and antisemitic. As if they had been waiting for a signal heralding a global intifada, large crowds flooded into the streets, taking up Islamists' age-old pledge to kill the Jews wherever they might be and establish dominance over the Holy Land.

The Biden administration may have been shocked to discover that the Middle East was not "quieter today than it had been for two decades," as National Security Advisor Jake Sullivan had declared it, with unfortunate timing, in late September 2023.[6] After almost three years of their stewardship, the region was in fact even more dangerous and volatile than it had been for a generation. In general, the administration's immediate response to the October 7 attacks was an expression of support for Israel as well as concern for Hamas's American victims who had been killed or taken hostage, setting the stage for close coordination between the Israel Defense Forces (IDF) and the U.S. Department of Defense as Israel prepared to respond militarily in Gaza.

Unfortunately, internal backlash against this support for Israel happened immediately. In the early morning hours of October 7, while the attacks were still going on, the State Department tweeted out a call for calm and restraint on both sides. No one was yet in possession of the full picture of what was happening, but the fact was clear that this was a generational act of aggression by Hamas, with devastating consequences for Israel. Pushback for this equivocating response from those whose first reaction was to support Israel was swift, which was followed by the standard Biden-administration cleanup: the tweet was deleted. But it was already emerging that there were elements in the administration, particularly in the White House and State Department, whose instinctive response to a Palestinian attack on Israel was to worry about Israeli retaliation against the Palestinians.

On October 18, as Israel initiated retaliatory military action against Hamas in Gaza, President Biden departed for Jerusalem. At first, the trip looked like a photo op for a commander in chief who had long professed support for the Jewish state, and perhaps even an opportunity to bring home American hostages. But while Air Force One was en route, *The New York Times* broke the news of an Israeli rocket strike on the Ahli Arab Hospital in Gaza City. The *Times* reported that photos and videos posted online, which the paper claimed to have verified, "showed bloodied and battered bodies, flames, grieving witnesses and the blankets, backpacks and mattresses of the dead and wounded littering the area around them."[7]

Outrage erupted immediately. The *Times* seemed to confirm that the IDF was not taking extreme measures to protect Gazan civilians as they had promised but were pursuing vengeance, treating all Palestinians as liable for October 7. There were rumors that the press pool on Air Force One was pressuring the president's staff to turn the plane around lest he be seen as culpable in the reported massacre.

Curiously enough, the Qatar-based news service Al Jazeera, usually sympathetic to Hamas, included in its report a statement by the Israeli government that it was investigating the incident but had no evidence that the IDF had been active in the area at the time of the strike. Al Jazeera was at first an outlier as condemnations of Israel's brutality as well as the pictures and videos of devastation rapidly spread online. As the hours passed, however, more enterprising journalists started to notice that the source of much of the information was the Gazan Ministry of Health, which was of course a division of Hamas.

Investigators eventually determined that Israeli planes had not been in the vicinity of the Ahli Arab Hospital and that the rocket had struck a parking lot, not the hospital itself. Many of the images that had provoked such outrage were from stock footage of other disasters. In fact, the world was introduced to the Palestinian Islamic Jihad, Hamas's terrorist partner, which was revealed to be the culprit, as one of its rockets aimed at Israel had gone astray. *The New York Times* later admitted its original reporting had been erroneous but excused itself on the grounds that reporting in Gaza is "difficult."[8] In the meantime, protests erupted at Israeli and U.S. embassies around the world and the flames of antisemitism were fanned into massive fireballs that have yet to be extinguished.

To the president's credit and the relief of those who value the U.S.–Israel alliance, he did not turn his plane around based on *The New York Times*'s erroneous reporting. But a mere ten days after the October 7 attacks, the damage to Israel's reputation was done. Global opinion had transformed the Jewish state from victim to aggressor—and oppressor and colonizer—in this conflict.

Biden's visit received generally positive reviews both in Israel and the United States. In his public remarks at Tel Aviv University, he started out on the right note:

> Hamas committed atrocities that recall the worst ravages of ISIS, unleashing pure, unadulterated evil upon the world. There is no rationalizing it, no excusing it. Period. The brutality we saw would have cut deep anywhere in the world, but it cuts deeper here in Israel. October 7th…a sacred Jewish holiday, became the deadliest day for the Jewish people since the Holocaust. It has brought to the surface painful memories and scars left by a millennia [sic] of anti-Semitism and the genocide of the Jewish people. The world watched then, it knew, and the world did nothing. We will not stand by and do nothing again. Not today, not tomorrow, not ever. To those who are living in limbo waiting desperately to learn the fate of loved ones, especially to families of the hostages: You're not alone. We're working with partners throughout the region, pursuing every avenue to bring home those who are being held captive by Hamas. I can't speak publicly about all the details, but let me assure you: For me as the American president, there is no higher priority than the release and safe return of all these hostages.[9]

But in recalling America's similar experience on September 11, 2001, Biden also struck a discordant note: "Justice must be done. But I caution this: While you feel that rage, don't be consumed by it. After 9/11 we were enraged in the United States. While we sought justice and got justice, we also made mistakes."[10]

The President's insinuation that George W. Bush's response to 9/11 was too knee-jerk and violent—rather than measured and proportionate

—was also an effort to shift blame from himself for the catastrophic surrender of Afghanistan in August 2021 by suggesting that shameful failure was caused by mistakes made at the outset. Given that in 2001 then-Senator Joe Biden was closely involved in the Congressional response to the Al-Qaeda attacks and must have known better, this is a curious piece of revisionist history. In the shock and horror that followed 9/11, all Americans were frantic to retaliate, and while President Bush famously promised the New York City first responders that the terrorists would "hear all of us soon," he did not in fact act precipitously.

The Bush administration, which had not been remotely prepared for an invasion of Afghanistan, actually took more than a month to ready its response, delaying against almost overwhelming political pressure to "do something."[11] But prudence paid dividends. The original invasion of Afghanistan, Operation Enduring Freedom, was something of an improvisational military operation that used both conventional and unconventional means, took advantage of local and international partnerships, and was masterfully executed by the brave servicemen and -women of the U.S. armed forces. By November, Kabul fell and rule of the government-designated Foreign Terrorist Organization (FTO), the Taliban, was ended.

Many books have been and will be written about the two decades that followed, but the suggestion that the well-prepared, overwhelming, and successful campaign against the point of origin of the 9/11 attacks was somehow an inappropriate model for Israel after October 7 defies logic. Mistakes—and there were plenty—came after, and Israel could indeed learn from the failed attempts to impose democracy on a tribal society, and the impulse on the part of the United States to do everything on our own on the grounds that the U.S. military could do so much better, acting solo. They might also take a lesson from America powerlessness to eradicate the intractable corruption and drug epidemic in Afghanistan.

But above all, Israel should learn from Biden's humiliating surrender of Afghanistan in August 2021, leaving our own infrastructure and equipment behind to be used against us in the future. That no one was ever held accountable for this failure, or for the loss of thirteen heroes via incompetence at Abbey Gate in Kabul, or for the false strike in an attempt to retaliate for them, which killed innocent Afghan children, remains a stain on our nation. And the whole episode emboldened America's adversaries around the world, including Iran, provoking outbursts such as the October 7 attacks.

The Kids Are Not All Right

OPPOSITION TO PRESIDENT BIDEN'S support for Israel soon intensified within the administration itself, causing him quickly to retreat from the messaging of his Israel visit. Many appointees, both career and political, had been overtly pro-Palestinian and tacitly anti-Israel from the beginning in January 2021, restoring funding to the Palestinian Authority and related U.N. agencies, prioritizing engagement with the Islamic Republic of Iran, and downgrading the relationship with Israel, especially after Benjamin Netanyahu became prime minister again in 2022.

The original October 7 State Department tweet established an unfortunate pattern for the administration's messaging: a statement opening with unequivocal commitment to Israel that then calls for the Jewish state to show restraint in its response.[12] This formulation gives an impression of the two sides is equal but puts the burden on Israel, the stronger party, to respond to an unprovoked and savage attack with measured reason.

The suggestion of moral equivalence fosters the Palestinians' conviction that global support for them, especially in the United States, is as strong as support for Israel, encouraging their resistance in the hope that one day America will cease to support Israel. Even more insidiously, it suggests that the terrorism that Palestinians, including but not limited to Hamas, deploy is a legitimate tactic that can lead to rewards—even to statehood.

The staff at both the State Department and the White House who had implemented the pro-Palestinian policies were dismayed by the president's support of the Israeli military operation in Gaza, which gathered steam in November 2023. In the days after the Ahli Arab Hospital incident, Josh Paul, who worked in the State Department bureau that oversees the transfer of military equipment abroad, announced he was resigning because he no longer felt the good he was doing outweighed the harm.[13] Whatever the merits of his position, at least Paul did the correct thing. Unelected staffers who disagree with the president have only one honorable course of action if, having expressed their dissent through the proper channels, they feel they can no longer serve: resign. And if they refuse to do so, they should be fired.[14]

But Paul was the only official who was willing to own up to his opposition to the Biden policy publicly in the aftermath of October 7. The rest remained anonymous—and in their jobs. The predictable leaks began, not surprisingly to *The New York Times,* which reported on November 14 that some five hundred administration officials across forty departments and agencies had signed an internal letter of protest opposing the administration's policy.[15] This was followed by reports of "listening sessions" at the White House and State Department, in which emotionally distressed staffers could express their grievances.[16] There was a public protest outside the White House itself, led by Josh Paul, but all the other protesters wore masks to hide their identities.[17] Finally, there were rumors of a day of protest organized by "Feds For Peace" on which concerned staff would collectively refuse to work.[18] A minor snowstorm canceled work that day for federal employees in the District of Columbia, and the plan was never revived, especially as civil servants were informed that unscheduled leave might be construed as protesting official U.S. policies, something they are not permitted to do in their roles as government employees.

Indoctrination Nation

THE DARKLY AMUSING FRAGILITY of these administration staffers was a preview of a nationwide problem that would pose a political conundrum for Biden. Beginning with "Critical Race Theory" in the late 1980s, cultural Marxism has gone on a thirty-year march through Western higher education and effectively banished all opposing viewpoints. Moving beyond orthodox Marxism's preoccupation with economics and class, cultural Marxists, as Mike Gonzalez and Katharine Gorka explain, believe that the revolution they seek requires

> cultural indoctrination, dismantling society's existing cultural narrative and instilling a new one.... Where the leftist of yore spoke of saving the working class or the proletariat, the twenty-first-century leftist speaks of the "marginalized" or the "members of underserved communities."... Today's cultural Marxists use race, sex, climate, or any number of other social issues to instill in the young a sense of grievance against the existing system and thus stoke an urge to reject tradition and opt for radical change.[19]

The young people who had flocked to join the Biden administration and implement his pro-Palestinian—and ultimately pro-Iranian—policies had been educated by a generation of progressive professors who were themselves the intellectual descendants of the pro-communist radicals of the 1960s. Their indoctrination from childhood into the cultural-Marxist construct of the "oppressors" versus the "oppressed" has reflexively supported the Palestinians as the oppressed party in the conflict with Israel, consigning the Jewish state, but also Jews around the world, to the category of "oppressors." Flowing naturally from this argument, if Israel is thus inherently racist and colonial, then antisemitism is not bigotry but the morally just position. It's also fashionable, especially if one dons a black-and-white keffiyeh (made in China and available for less than twenty dollars on Amazon) in solidarity with the Palestinians. Combined with a COVID mask to hide the identity of the not-so-innocent, it's the new radical chic.[20]

Two years before October 7, Vice President Kamala Harris, however inadvertently, provided a window into this growing problem. She was at George Mason University to talk about voting rights when a student informed her that "just a few days ago there were funds allocated to continue backing Israel, which hurts my heart because it's an ethnic genocide and a displacement of people, the same that happened in America, and I'm sure you're aware of this."[21] The statement leveled the libelous charge of genocide—a war crime—against Israel, and perpetuates the lie that the Jews are a foreign irritant and not indigenous to the Holy Land, and as such should be expelled. Even more egregiously, she lumped America into this libel.

The vice president of the United States might respond forcefully to such unfounded accusations even while celebrating the free speech that allowed the student to voice her opinion, but Harris did no such thing. She instead responded that she was "glad" the student had raised the point and added, "this is about the fact that your voice, your perspective, your experience, your truth, should not be suppressed and it must be heard, right? And one of the things we're fighting for in a democracy, right?"

Harris no doubt believed she was speaking the student's language, but the second-highest elected official in the United States was not doing undergraduates any favors by encouraging them to believe they can imagine the truth to be anything they want. Rather than gloss over pernicious bigotry, Harris would have done better to treat the George Mason student to a history lesson on what such attacks have led to in the past. But instead, she left the impression that the student had made a valid point.

The months following the Hamas attacks revealed the intensity and scope of this problem, especially in America's universities. An anti-Israel protest erupted at Columbia University in New York on October 10, soon followed by campus protests across the country. While there were broader urban demonstrations in cities such as London, New York, and Los Angeles, the campus protests proved more durable and deep-rooted.

A few high-profile philanthropists, such as the Harvard alum Bill Ackman and the University of Pennsylvania's Huntsman family, outraged at this explosion of antisemitism, announced their intention to cut off support for these institutions, but they were outliers. Most trustees and donors stuck with their universities because they were not unsympathetic to the radicals that they have known all too well for decades.

Cracks in Biden's Base

IN THE CRITICAL RACE THEORY construct of the Middle East conflict, roles are clearly defined: Jews in Israel are colonial oppressors who have been externally and illegally imposed on the oppressed indigenous Arab population. One peer-reviewed academic essay on the topic, "Race, Palestine, and International Law," summarized it thusly:

> In 1922, the League of Nations inscribed the goal of establishing a settler colony in Palestine for the Jewish people—in denial of the national self-determination of the Indigenous Arab population—in public international law. The Palestine Mandate juridically erased the national status of the Palestinian people by: (1) framing the Arabs as incapable of self-rule; (2) heightening the significance of establishing a Jewish national home; and (3) distinguishing Palestine from the other Class A mandates for possessing religious significance that exceeded the interests of any single national group. A century later, the still-unresolved "question" of Palestine remains central to struggles for anti-racism and anti-colonialism in international law. This essay revisits two flashpoints in the tangled history of Palestine and international law, where questions of race and racism have been central: first, ongoing debates over the regime and crime of apartheid; and second, the now-repudiated U.N. General Assembly Resolution 3379, recognizing Zionism as a form of racism and racial discrimination. Both stories demonstrate the importance of understanding race and colonialism as conjoined concepts, neither of which can be properly understood in isolation from the other.[22]

According to this narrative, Israel is inherently racist and colonial—and, most importantly, illegal according to international law—the three things that American students in higher education are taught across all disciplines are inherently evil and therefore deserving of resistance by any means. And lest one think an essay such as this one is on the fringes of esoteric academia, let it sink in that while it originally appeared in the *American Journal of International Law*, it was also published online by Cambridge University Press on March 28, 2023, as part of their "CambridgeCore" curriculum, a curated collection of readings that is used broadly around the world. Little wonder then, that students being indoctrinated in such texts from authoritative sources instinctively responded to October 7 with support of the Palestinians, and with opposition to Jews, as had been the plan all along.

As the presidential-election year of 2024 proceeded, the crisis in the Middle East presented President Biden with an acute domestic political dilemma. On the one hand, Muslim Americans overwhelmingly supported the Palestinian cause and opposed American support for Israel. While accounting for a small percentage of the overall U.S. population— just 1.1 percent in 2017[23]—Muslim Americans are highly concentrated in critical counties in the swing state of Michigan, with its fifteen contested electoral votes. Donald Trump won Michigan in 2016 by a narrow margin, but then Joe Biden took the state in 2020 by less than 3 percentage points. Michigan would once again be critical in 2024, and to prevail Biden would need to win the Muslim vote overwhelmingly. The Democratic primary in February was not encouraging. Biden won handily with no real opposition, but more than 13 percent voted "uncommitted" in protest over the war in Gaza. These were a hundred thousand votes that Kamala Harris, now the Democratic candidate for president would need come November.

The youth vote presented a larger problem. Approximately 10 percent more of the eighteen-to-twenty-nine-year-old demographic turned out in 2020 than in 2016, and 69 percent of them voted for Biden, while 35 percent voted for Trump.[24] Having pandered to this group with a progressive climate policy, student-loan forgiveness, and pro-abortion activism, Biden and Harris considered young votes locked up at the beginning of October 2023. But that was called into question after the attack, as support for the Palestinians was much higher among these voters than among older Americans who have not been educated according to Critical Race Theory's dictates. In the spring of 2024, the young-voter demographic became increasingly radicalized.

The Legacy of Terrorism

THE WAR IN GAZA has been, to quote former Secretary of Defense Donald Rumsfeld, a "long, hard slog," but the Israelis have been making progress, especially after the offensive into Rafah on the Egyptian border. Hamas has followed its standard practice of using the Palestinian people as an extension of its military, making high civilian casualties predictable and indeed desirable from Hamas's perspective as a propaganda device. The Biden administration has gone to great lengths to make a distinction between Hamas and the rest of the people living in Gaza, but it is a distinction without a difference. The harsh reality is that the Palestinians in Gaza broadly adhere to the terms of Hamas's charter, which calls for the elimination of Israel and the establishment of a single Palestinian state in its place. Not negotiation and not coexistence, but rather the extermination of the Jews. Refusing to acknowledge this fact and failing to change it will only lead to more violence and terrorism—not to mention more suffering for the Palestinian people. As Israeli Prime Minister Benjamin Netanyahu has said, "For us, every uninvolved civilian who is hurt is a tragedy. For Hamas it's a strategy."[25]

Hamas, supported by the Muslim Brotherhood, emerged in 1987 as an organized political force in Gaza, representing the overtly Islamist faction of the Palestinians.[26] Although designated as a Foreign Terrorist Organization by the United States in 1997, however ironically, Hamas's rule over Gaza was largely the unintended result of U.S. policy. After the successful invasions of Afghanistan and then Iraq following 9/11, the George W. Bush administration made refashioning these countries into liberal democracies the cornerstone of its counterterrorism strategy. The rationale was extremely appealing, especially to Americans. In his second inaugural address, President Bush identified democracy as the cure for all that ailed us.[27] Democracies encourage tolerance and acceptance, not extremism and hate. And, according to the president, democracies do not attack each other. If we had democracy, we would, ergo, have peace.

History offered some support for this line of reasoning. After the Second World War, for example, the imperial aggressor powers of Japan and Germany were liberalized and became two of America's great democratic and capitalist allies. Additional attacks from them seemed unimaginable. Even Russia, which as the head of the Soviet Union had been a deadly adversary through the long decades of the Cold War, appeared to be heading toward a freer system following the fall of the Berlin Wall in 1989, and was counted on to provide counterterrorism cooperation to the United States after 9/11.

If democracy had tamed such formidable foes as these, the idea of applying it to the intractable and alien ideology of radical Islam was attractive. The Bush administration believed that by promoting democracies across the Middle East, we would be bringing a better future to the people of the region as well as increasing the security of the United States.

At first, the plan seemed successful, as "freedom donkeys" carried ballots into the hinterlands of Afghanistan and apparently enthusiastic voters displayed their purple-stained index fingers for the Western media. But sectarian challenges, corruption, and insurgent violence quickly darkened the picture, particularly in Iraq, which threatened President Bush's legacy. His administration started to look elsewhere in the Middle East for opportunities, including two countries that had not played a major role in his first term: Iran and Israel.

While some senior members of the administration, notably Vice President Dick Cheney and Secretary Rumsfeld, had advocated for turning to Iran after Afghanistan, President Bush decided to tackle Iraq instead. When that project began to sour, the appetite for further military intervention diminished. Spearheaded by Secretary of State Condoleezza Rice, the policy became one of democratization in Iran by encouragement and engagement to win hearts and minds, not invasion.

Hoping for a major diplomatic victory for the embattled president, Secretary Rice engaged more closely with the Israel–Palestinian issue. President Clinton had tried to broker a deal at the end of his second term, but the chairman of the Palestine Liberation Organization, Yasser Arafat, refused the generous terms offered by Israeli Prime Minister Ehud Barack. Arafat's rejection of the offer, which included statehood and promised a prosperous and secure life for the Palestinians, was an ominous indication of the absolutist mindset of his people. Not content with a Palestinian state, Arafat was intent on eradicating Israel.

The Bush administration decided to address the problem of Gaza, then home to both Jews and Palestinians and heavily monitored by the IDF. In an attempt to mollify the Palestinian Authority, led by Mahmoud Abbas, it encouraged the Israeli prime minister, Ariel Sharon, to evacuate all the Jews from the Gaza Strip and remove the IDF. Elections would then take place in short order, giving the Palestinians who remained a government of their own choosing and leading, according to the logic of the Bush administration, to peace.

The Gazans duly voted, but by an overwhelming margin they chose not a liberal, secular slate of leaders who would develop civic institutions and encourage economic development but representatives of the radical terrorist group Hamas, which was strongly supported by Iran. Instead of solving the problem of terrorism in Gaza, the overeager promotion of and faith in democracy had brought to power a group that had been designated a Foreign Terrorist Organization by the United States since 1997.

Once installed, Hamas transformed Gaza into a terrorist fiefdom, the purpose of which was to resist and ultimately attack Israel. This unhappy state of affairs had in no way been inevitable. Gaza has everything necessary to be a beautiful and prosperous place. The international community is filled with wealthy donors eager to provide resources for development. But that was not what Hamas wanted. More importantly, that was not what the majority of the Palestinians living in Gaza wanted.

In the years after the 2006 election, Hamas infiltrated every aspect of life in Gaza—military, political, and humanitarian. Its first priority was military capacity, so most resources went to militants and weapons to attack Israel. Every few years, it would amass enough of both to start a conflict, and when Israel responded with vastly superior force, Hamas would survive to fight another day owing to the protection of institutions such as the United Nations. Insisting that Israel act with restraint, these international organizations ensured that the deadly pattern would be repeated.

Hamas also controlled Gaza's medical facilities and schools. Since these were unappetizing targets for Israeli retaliation, Gaza's flagship institution was Al-Shifa Hospital, the most modern medical center in the Strip.

Originally a sturdy British army barracks, Al-Shifa had been converted into a hospital after the British relinquished their mandate to govern the area in 1946. Attempting to improve living conditions for the Palestinians, the government of Israel had modernized Al-Shifa in the 1980s, turning it into the most sophisticated structure in Gaza. On coming to power, Hamas took advantage of the facilities at Al-Shifa and established its headquarters in the basement, assuming (correctly) that the Israelis would be reluctant to bomb a hospital, especially one they had recently renovated.[28] Al-Shifa exemplified the larger problem of Hamas in Gaza—it couldn't be eradicated because it had become embedded in the very infrastructure that was supposed to keep Gazans alive.

The United Nations Relief and Works Agency presents an even more intractable problem. Set up in 1949 to provide humanitarian assistance to Palestinian refugees after the establishment of the state of Israel, UNRWA is involved with health care, social services, and—of particular importance in Gaza—education. Hamas saw the control of education as vital for its survival, so it completely co-opted UNRWA, embedding Hamas members in its ranks as both teachers and administrators. Hamas's genocidal mission to eradicate Israel found its way into everything from textbooks to cartoons to school plays, while UNRWA's physical facilities were opened for weapons storage and tunnel digging. The United States is the single largest funder of UNRWA.

The American Hamas Support Networks

HAMAS'S TACTICS AND BELIEFS are defended and even celebrated throughout U.S. higher education as legitimate tools of "resistance," so that's where the militants turned for support as Israel moved toward a decisive military victory over Hamas in the spring of 2024. The pro-Hamas demonstrations and antisemitic attacks on campus that had abated for some months suddenly returned to the headlines as the IDF closed in on Rafah, Hamas's last stronghold in Gaza, where the bulk of its remaining four thousand fighters were thought to be holed up along with more than one million Palestinian refugees and, possibly, one hundred or so Jewish hostages.

Columbia University, where one of the first protest "encampments" appeared, was ground zero in this effort. Characterized by the distinctively uniform green tents, these installations cropped up on campuses from George Washington University to UCLA, hardened against dispersal with increasingly sophisticated constructions out of plywood and chains. When the protesters at Columbia forgot to bring food and had to go hungry, the University refused to provide catering, and supply chains for sustenance sprang up. Hamilton Hall in the center of the Columbia campus was briefly seized in an attempt to disrupt the operations of the university. At UCLA, a massive police intervention was required to break up its encampment.

Almost universally, the tenured faculty of these academic institutions sided with the protesters. As classes and then exams were canceled or went virtual for the broader student bodies, professors joined the demonstrations, frequently donning the uniform of keffiyeh and COVID mask in solidarity. When some students at the University of North Carolina were suspended for their disruptive behavior, faculty withheld grades for all students until the university agreed to lift the suspensions.[29]

Professors and administrators also broadly supported negotiations with the protesters that would address a standard menu of demands. These negotiations emerged at institutions as diverse as Rutgers

University in New Jersey and Northwestern University in suburban Chicago, and included teaching positions for Palestinian professors from Gaza, scholarships for Palestinian students, and so-called "Boycott, Divest, and Sanction" (BDS) policies that would prohibit university investments in companies with financial exposure to Israel.

Eager to end the protests before graduation, many institutions agreed to these demands, however questionable their legality or the ability to implement them. In June 2023, for instance, the Supreme Court had issued a decision in two related cases, *Students for Fair Admissions, Inc. (SFFA) v. President & Fellows of Harvard College* and *SFFA v. University of North Carolina*, finding that admission decisions based on racial criteria were unconstitutional.[30] And some thirty-eight states had adopted laws against this sort of forced divestment based on exposure to Israel. Illinois, home to Northwestern, for example, adopted anti–boycott, divest, and sanction (BDS) legislation in 2015. If the University actually enforced the divestment requirement of the protesters, state grant money for research could be held at risk. But the impossibility of their demands did not deter the students from making them or the administrators from agreeing at least to explore complying with them, as if their institutions exist outside the rule of law that governs normal Americans.

In an echo of the Black Lives Matter riots of 2020, the pro-Hamas protesters also targeted statues of the American founding fathers that had long been fixtures on many of these campuses. At the University of Pennsylvania, the bronze statue of Benjamin Franklin that has stood before College Hall since 1939 was festooned with a keffiyeh and a Palestinian flag. But special venom was reserved for the bronze copy of Jean-Antoine Houdon's eighteenth-century *George Washington* at the university that bears his name in America's capital city. Not content with wrapping a keffiyeh around the face as if the statue were part of the riot, protesters plastered the body of the first president with stickers reading "Free Palestine" and "Free Gaza" and spray-painted "Genocidal Warmonger University" on the base.[31] The message was clear: The leader of the American Revolution must be transformed into a member of the

Palestinian resistance, his own identity and history obliterated. The students of George Washington University were putting the Marxist theory of their professors into practice with a vengeance.

The attacks on the founding fathers went hand in hand with attacks on American flags, demonstrating that these protests were aimed not at the government of Israel but were instead a broader attack on anything identified as an oppressor. Mob burnings of American as well as Israeli flags became a standard component of the demonstrations. The prominent American flag in Harvard Yard and the one at the University of Chicago were lowered and replaced by the Palestinian flag, an action uncontested by campus police.

But the most dramatic of these episodes took place at the University of North Carolina at Chapel Hill, where the large American flag flying over campus was removed and replaced with a Palestinian flag. When police tried to reinstall the Stars and Stripes, protesters fought to tear it down again. This time, however, a group of UNC fraternity brothers, who had come to the protests to try to understand them better, intervened. Pelted with garbage and threatened with violence, the young men defended the flag until the protesters were dispersed. The spontaneous patriotism of the so-called "UNC Frat Bros" struck a nerve with the American people, who flooded their GoFundMe account with donations. They originally hoped to raise a few thousand dollars for a party to celebrate their victory but wound up receiving more than $500,000, which will largely go to a pro-American charity. While the ugly antisemitism on American campuses revealed by the demonstrations since October 7, 2023, is clearly part of the larger pro-Hamas campaign, the events at UNC proved what a little courage can do.

Information Wars

HAMAS AND ITS ENABLERS had a sophisticated and seasoned communications plan ready to push out to the global media, establishing the Palestinians as the victims of Israeli aggression, the events of October 7 notwithstanding. That original tweet from the State Department's Office of Palestinian Affairs set the stage for a campaign to delegitimize Israel for being inhumane and indiscriminately punishing Palestinian civilians. The effort began with the *danse macabre* around the Gaza City hospital, and quickly gained steam. Getting humanitarian aid into Gaza, rather than eradicating Hamas and securing the release of hostages held by them, became an international obsession and the top priority for the Biden administration.

Less than a month after the Hamas attack, Secretary of State Antony Blinken declared on one of his many visits to the region, "When I see [a] Palestinian boy or girl [pulled] from the wreckage of the building, it hits me in the gut. This is hitting everyone. I see my own children in their faces. And as human beings—how can any of us not feel the same way?"[32] Yet millions seem unable to see their own children in the Jewish babies slaughtered on October 7 and those still held by Hamas in Gaza's underground maze of terror tunnels.

The anti-Israel propaganda campaign held the Jewish state responsible for providing food and services to the Palestinians in the Strip, even as Hamas disrupted the flow of relief. The IDF found itself in the impossible position of trying to execute a military operation against Hamas while protecting and supplying the civilians among whom Hamas had embedded itself. Never before, in the history of warfare, has the international community demanded that a combatant in a hot war provide relief to its adversary. Indeed, it's impossible to imagine the United States providing relief to Japan in the aftermath of Pearl Harbor, or the United Kingdom providing food and fuel to the Germans during the Blitz. Yet the international community, spearheaded by the United Nations, the European Union, and the Biden administration's Secretary of State Blinken and USAID Administrator Samantha Power, demanded that Israel do just that.

International condemnation for Israel's action in Gaza was intensified by the assumption that the broader population in Gaza had no culpability for the October 7 attacks. The reality, unfortunately, is that the roughly 1,500 terrorists who burst out of Gaza into Israel did not come from nowhere. Savage killers are produced in those numbers by indoctrinating them with genocidal hatred from a very early age. And that indoctrination was carried out with the tacit agreement, if not the active participation, of their Palestinian parents and teachers, not all of whom were card-carrying members of Hamas.

The former Israeli prime minister Golda Meir reflected ruefully, "When peace comes, we will perhaps in time be able to forgive the Arabs for killing our sons, but it will be harder for us to forgive them for having forced us to kill their sons. Peace will come when the Arabs will love their children more than they hate us."[33] The recorded phone calls of triumphant terrorists bragging to their jubilant parents on October 7 about how many Jews they had killed were a grim reminder of the real Palestinian mindset.

Then there was the case of UNRWA, the bespoke agency dedicated to serving the Palestinians, while the other hundred million displaced peoples of the world must share the attention of the United Nations High Commission for Refugees. With pretensions to the moral high ground as supposedly the only effective channel of humanitarian aid to Gaza and the West Bank, UNRWA commands, unchallenged, the bounty of Western nations afraid of radicalizing the next generation of Palestinians.

The problem is that UNRWA, completely committed to the Palestinian cause and equally hostile to Israel, is not interested in deradicalization. When it was revealed that Hamas was storing arms and militants in the agency's facilities, even hospitals and schools, and that employees of the agency were actively participating in Hamas activities, UNRWA apologists dismissed the culprits as a few bad apples who should not distract attention from the agency's mission. Even when the agency's director-general, Philippe Lazzarini, was confronted with evidence that a dozen agency employees had participated in the murderous rampage on October 7, he refused to change the agency's direction or resign.[34] In fact, Lazzarini used the occasion to call for more European funding for UNRWA.

Israel, for its part, has no incentive to exacerbate the hardships of Palestinians in Gaza, even if they are complicit with Hamas, if only to avoid the inevitable PR damage. What set this operation in Gaza apart, however, was Israel's refusal to allow accusations of humanitarian abuses of the Palestinians to dictate its policy as it had in the past. This approach has allowed Israel to make considerably more gains on the battlefield than in previous engagements, but those gains have come at a price.

In early 2024, President Biden shifted the focus of his public rhetoric on Gaza to the humanitarian plight of the Palestinians. Expressions of solidarity with Israel were correspondingly tempered. Oddly, the State Department decided to outsource its humanitarian work in Gaza to celebrity chef José Andrés, whose nongovernmental charity operation, World Central Kitchen (WCK), has focused on providing food and water to populations in need for more than a decade. Much of Andrés's work may well be admirable, notably in Haiti, but in Gaza, WCK made the mistake of focusing on Israel as the problem rather than Hamas.

WCK found a willing partner in the State Department, which was not developing many creative ideas to get humanitarian aid into Gaza without benefitting Hamas (spoiler alert: there aren't any). But on Andrés's recommendation the concept was developed for a so-called "humanitarian pier" in Gaza—a new structure that would be used exclusively to get assistance into the Strip. This idea was so appealing to USAID administrator Power that it made it all the way into President Biden's State of the Union Speech on March 8, 2024:

> The United States has been leading international efforts to get more humanitarian assistance into Gaza. Tonight, I'm directing the U.S. military to lead an emergency mission to establish a temporary pier in the Mediterranean on the coast of Gaza that can receive large shipments carrying food, water, medicine, and temporary shelters. No U.S. boots will be on the ground. This temporary pier would enable a massive increase in the amount of humanitarian assistance getting into Gaza every day. But Israel must also do its part. Israel must allow more aid into Gaza and ensure that humanitarian workers aren't caught in the crossfire.[35]

Chef Andrés applauded joyfully from the gallery as the personal guest of former Speaker of the House Nancy Pelosi, and no one questioned the fact that the Biden administration had apparently put its Gaza policy in the hands of a celebrity chef. But executing this ambitious plan would be enormously complicated. How would this new pier operate separately and securely from the existing Gaza pier? If there were no U.S. boots on the ground, how would it be protected? How would Hamas be prevented from attacking it or seizing the aid that came from it? And wasn't the real need for additional truckloads of aid crossing by land, which had been hampered by Hamas's attacks?

These questions were never answered. The pier became operational on May 17, 2024, and the aid started to move to much fanfare. Just days later, however, the Pentagon deputy press secretary quietly announced that while hundreds of tons of aid had arrived, there was no way to ascertain if any of it had actually reached any Palestinian civilians, and the Department of Defense would be looking for alternative routes to deliver it.[36] After washing ashore in rough seas, the pier was finally dismantled in late July, just two months into its mission.[37]

Meanwhile, the perilous famine in Gaza that had been predicted in the media since October 2023 failed to materialize. If there had been any credible accounts of mass starvation, they would have been pushed by Hamas to its regular contacts at *The New York Times* and elsewhere. But even so, the political imperative to "do something" about humanitarian suffering following any Israeli incursion into the Strip became increasingly intense in the United States over the course of the spring of 2024.

Hamas's Useful Idiots

THE NUMBERS OF CIVILIAN casualties in Gaza, especially women and children, reported by the United Nations seemed chilling. Estimates issued by the Hamas-controlled Government Media Office (GMO) in Gaza City put the figures in the tens of thousands. These numbers gained broad credence because the Biden administration used them publicly and repeatedly. In February 2024, President Biden and then Secretary of Defense Lloyd Austin cited the figure of twenty-five to thirty thousand, which had been put out by the same Gaza Ministry of Health that had falsely reported an Israeli strike on the Gaza City Hospital at the beginning of the conflict. When questioned, the White House and Defense Department admitted the Hamas-supplied numbers could not be verified but did nothing to correct the record or suggest that the true number might be lower. The president repeated Hamas's figures in his State of the Union address.

In the first week of May, the United Nations Office for the Coordination of Humanitarian Affairs (OCHA) published the GMO figures of some nine thousand Palestinian women and fifteen thousand children killed in Gaza after October 7, ostensibly confirming the Biden administration's estimate. But just two days later, OCHA halved its official estimate to reflect the numbers reported by the Gaza Ministry of Health (also controlled by Hamas).[38] No apology or explanation was offered, and the fact of the matter appeared to be that no one, not the White House and least of all the various factions of Hamas, had accurate numbers for civilian casualties in Gaza.

It should surprise no one that Hamas invents whatever suits its propaganda campaign to demonize Israel, but what has been shocking in the current crisis is the willingness of not only the usual apologists such as the United Nations but also the most senior members of the Biden administration, including the president himself, to amplify and legitimize its lies. Hamas has been masterful in its ability to change its image from the terrorists who attacked Israel on October 7 to the victims of Israel's retaliatory aggression, but it has also had a lot of help.

As the months passed, President Biden quietly started to distance himself from the ongoing hostage crisis in Gaza, undermining one of the most powerful counternarratives to Hamas's propaganda campaign. For a period, the United States could use the hostages' safety as leverage to keep Israel from moving into the southern Gaza city of Rafah and finishing the operation for fear of additional Palestinian casualties, but Hamas's own refusal to make a deal eventually made this appeal ineffective.

Early in the war, President Biden had been eager to claim success when Jewish hostages were exchanged for finite ceasefires and the release of hundreds of Hamas prisoners. During his Christmas vacation on Nantucket, he even spoke publicly on the subject.[39] But as the months dragged on and Hamas rejected additional offers for more releases, the administration scarcely mentioned the hostages, who quietly dropped out of the headlines, including the Americans held in Gaza.

The president's concern about the damage the Gaza issue was doing to his standing with young voters was apparent in his graduation address at Morehead College in Atlanta in May 2024. In the middle of his heavily autobiographical speech, he turned for a moment to the war in the Middle East, beginning with an acknowledgment of "Hamas's vicious attack on Israel." But he devoted the rest of his remarks to the "humanitarian crisis in Gaza," suggesting that the most important question is "What rights do the Palestinian people have?" He had barely a word about the hostages, even the Americans, and never mentioned "terrorism" or Iran's role in the attacks.[40] In other words, the president of the United States was perfectly on message—Hamas's message.

Hamas leaders knew quite well that they were winning global opinion—even when they lost on the battlefield—and steadfastly refused to make any concessions. In early June, after trying for months for a negotiated release for more hostages, the IDF executed a daring raid on Nuseirat, a U.N. refugee camp in central Gaza, that freed four of them. Three of the hostages were being held in the home of a former Al Jazeera reporter, while the fourth, a female named Noa Argamani, was captive in the home of a wealthy local family.[41] Noa's abduction from the Nova Music Festival on October 7 had been filmed by the terrorists who took her and widely broadcast her kidnapping, making her one of the faces of the young women who had been taken hostage.

Despite the joy in Israel at their return, international attention quickly turned to blaming Israel for the Palestinians killed in the raid. Hamas claimed it was hundreds, which was widely accepted without verification. Vice President Kamala Harris, speaking to Michigan Democratic Party members, was almost booed off the stage by Hamas supporters for mentioning the hostage release, even as she pandered to the audience by detailing her concerns about civilian casualties. National Security Advisor Jake Sullivan took it a step further and declared any day that saw the loss of Palestinian life "is another horrible, awful, tragic day," even if innocent Israeli hostages come home.[42]

Lawfare

ISRAEL'S OBVIOUS ADVANTAGE OVER Hamas is being a sovereign and successful democratic nation with membership in various international bodies, including the United Nations. The Palestinians, by contrast, are a group of people, not a state, and Hamas is a terrorist organization, not a legitimate governing institution. In evaluating its own national interests, the United States must not lose sight of this distinction, however much it desires to improve the lot of the Palestinian people. Yet in the months following October 7, 2023, the Biden administration's actions showed a remarkable disregard for Israeli sovereignty and suggested that the international community should pretend that the Palestinian people were represented by something like a state regardless of their behavior on October 7.

For example, President Biden tried to meddle in Israeli politics by suggesting that its freely elected conservative government was part of the problem. When Benjamin Netanyahu returned to the premiership in 2022, Biden called him "my friend for decades,"[43] but the American president has subsequently tried to make the Israeli prime minister the scapegoat for everything that has gone wrong in the region and the main obstacle to the hostages' return.

The Biden administration first challenged the legitimacy of the Israeli government in late February 2024, when Secretary of State Antony Blinken quietly reversed the State Department's policy on the legal status of Jewish settlements in West Bank, also known as Judea and Samaria.[44] In November 2019, Blinken's predecessor, Mike Pompeo, had himself reversed some forty years of bipartisan consensus that any Jewish building in the West Bank was "illegitimate" under international law. The United

States then maintained that any disputes over the construction should be resolved in Israeli, not international, courts. This new position on West Bank settlements, like the move of the U.S. embassy to Jerusalem, clarified the American view of Israeli sovereignty over the territory within its borders.

Just four months after October 7, desperate to make a conciliatory gesture to the Palestinians, Blinken stated that he concluded it was only Pompeo's opinion, not formal guidance, so they could simply revert to the policy of declaring the settlements illegitimate—a policy that had been an abject failure since 1978. The Biden administration's message was clear: international law, not Israeli law, should determine where Israeli citizens can build within Israel's borders, an echo of the legal arguments of proponents of Critical Race Theory.

As for the Palestinians, the Biden administration has tried mightily to distinguish between Hamas and the people who live in the Gaza Strip, as though it were only an unfortunate accident that the Palestinians there are ruled by Hamas. Yet these are the people who elected Hamas in the first place and continue to support both it and the terrorist attacks of October 7.[45]

In the months after the attacks, the Biden administration began to insinuate a similar distinction between the people of Israel and their duly elected government. Vice President Harris laid this formula out in March, declaring in an interview with CBS, "I think it is important to distinguish, or at least not conflate, the Israeli government with the Israeli people."[46] The assumption is that the Palestinians should not be considered responsible for the attacks of October 7 nor the Israelis for their government's response, as if the government of Israel were somehow imposed on Israelis, not elected by them—and that the majority of Israelis did not support their government's response, despite unambiguous polling to the contrary.

A few days later, Senate Majority Leader Chuck Schumer went a step further when he excoriated the Netanyahu government in a speech on the Senate floor, going so far as to declare it was time for new elections in Israel. He absolved the Palestinians of blame for the attack on Israel but castigated Israel for the humanitarian crisis in Gaza, saying, "We should not let the complexities of this conflict stop us from stating the plain truth: Palestinian civilians do not deserve to suffer for the sins of Hamas, and Israel has a moral obligation to do better." The only path to peace, Schumer asserted, is the two-state solution, and he went on to identify "four major obstacles standing in the way of two states": "Hamas, and the Palestinians who support and tolerate their evil ways. Radical right-wing Israelis in government and society. Palestinian Authority President Mahmoud Abbas. Israeli Prime Minister Benjamin Netanyahu." A two-state solution, in other words, will require not only new leadership for the Palestinian people but also a new government in Israel, shorn of those incorrigible conservatives: "At this critical juncture, I believe a new election is the only way to allow for a healthy and open decision-making process about the future of Israel, at a time when so many Israelis have lost their confidence in the vision and direction of their government."[47]

It was an astonishing public statement by the senior-most self-identified Jewish elected official in the United States. Hamas must have been delighted to see this fraying of the bonds between Jerusalem and Washington and to hear an American leader personally blaming Netanyahu for it. Harris and Schumer appeared to believe that if the prime minister were not ousted, it would call into question Israel's status as a democracy, and thus one of the core tenets of America's support for the Jewish state.

The same week that Harris and Schumer made their remarks, Secretary Blinken followed up on his action against the settlements with a more pointed set of sanctions on specific settlers he found problematic. Perhaps believing that the Biden administration had been a little too one-sided in its treatment of Hamas and Israel, the State Department placed sanctions on three Israeli settlers accused of "harassing and attacking Palestinians to pressure them to leave their land," wittingly or otherwise echoing the Hamas justification for October 7. As if the Israeli settlers' actions were comparable to Hamas's attacks, the administration followed up with sanctions on U.S. organizations that raised money for the settlers on the grounds that this was providing material support to sanctioned individuals.

This dangerous undermining of Israel and its citizens was combined with an effort to elevate the Palestinians in international organizations, primarily through the United Nations. On March 25, 2024, the United States, by abstaining from the vote, allowed the passage of U.N. Security Council Resolution (UNSCR) 2728, which demanded an immediate ceasefire in Gaza during Ramadan, the release of the hostages, and access to humanitarian aid in Gaza.[48]

In an unusual move, the Biden administration had originally proposed its own draft resolution for a ceasefire, which had been vetoed by Russia and China, so the U.S. position would seem not to have changed with the abstention. But 2728 differed from the U.S. proposal in two important respects. First, a condemnation of the attacks of October 7 as terrorist outrages against humanity—a condemnation that apparently prompted the Russian and Chinese vetoes—was removed. Second, while 2728 demanded the release of the hostages, it did not make the demand for a ceasefire contingent on their release. In other words, this Security Council resolution, though "deploring...all violence and hostilities against civilians, and all acts of terrorism," opened the door to a ceasefire without the release of the hostages—and the United States let it pass.

Sadly, the Biden administration can point to previous bipartisan American equivocations at the United Nations intended to persuade the Palestinians that the United States had not really taken a side in the conflict and was sincerely committed to their cause, while paying lip service to America's support for Israel. But such twisted logic, along with the canard that an abstention is somehow different than an affirmative vote, is too cute by half.

In the dying days of the George W. Bush administration in January 2009, President George W. Bush's then–Secretary of State Condoleezza Rice considered voting for UNSCR 1860, which the U.S. Mission to the

U.N. had helped draft during that round of violence provoked by Hamas. Like 2728, 1860 called for an immediate ceasefire and the facilitation of humanitarian aid to Gaza, while providing no security assurances to Israel. Rice ultimately abstained, and 1860 passed. The episode set an unfortunate Republican precedent that subsequent Democrat administrations have exploited.

In December 2016, this pattern repeated with UNSCR 2334 at the end of the Obama administration, which condemned the settlement activities of the "occupying power" Israel in the Palestinian territories, thus perpetuating the fantasy that there is an equivalency between the two parties. The then–U.S. Ambassador to the U.N. Samantha Power abstained, allowing the resolution to pass, with the cover that she was only doing what the Bush administration had done eight years earlier. None of these Security Council resolutions has materially reduced violence or produced peace in the Middle East, but they have all contributed to the counterproductive impression among the Palestinians that violence against Israel is somehow legitimate in the eyes of the United Nations—as is their support of the perpetuators of this violence, first and foremost Hamas.[49]

Based on this history, the Biden administration has increasingly relied on the United Nations to provide cover for their muddled policy towards the conflict. In May 2024, the U.N. General Assembly took up a resolution to make the Palestinians a full member of the United Nations. No entity that is not a nation-state has ever been a full member, and previous attempts have always been stymied by the United States. The Biden administration itself had done so on April 1 but noted, "Our vote does not reflect opposition to Palestinian statehood. Instead it is an acknowledgement that statehood will come only from a process that involves direct negotiations between the parties."[50] Will the United States continue to oppose membership for the Palestinians in the face of overwhelming support in the General Assembly (143 in favor, nine against, and twenty-five abstentions), as the Biden administration had already leaked their musings on ways to recognize a Palestinian entity absent such an agreement with Israel? At the time of this writing, that is still an open question.

These shifts in the U.S. stance toward Israel emboldened the International Criminal Court (ICC) prosecutor in May 2024 to accuse Prime Minister Benjamin Netanyahu and Defense Minister Yoav Gallant, both elected members of the Israeli Knesset as well as cabinet ministers, of war crimes and to request warrants for their arrest.[51] This announcement put the Biden administration and U.S. senators of both parties in a bind, as they had supported a similar finding against Russian President Vladimir Putin for his invasion of Ukraine and stated publicly that the ICC was the proper court in which to adjudicate such a charge. Neither the United States nor Israel is a signatory to the ICC, so the warrants would not be binding, but the action of the ICC emboldened the U.N. International Court of Justice (IJC) to demand that Israel halt its military offensive into the southern Gaza town of Rafah, a demand that the Biden administration had opposed. Since the United States and Israel are members of the United Nations, this decision may prove to have more teeth.

President Biden did at first publicly denounce the ICC recommendation to issue warrants. But just a few weeks after they were announced, the White House received an angry call from the actor George Clooney, whose wife Amal, a prominent human-rights lawyer, had publicly advised the ICC prosecutor who had issued the warrants.[52] Clooney, who was to be hosting a major political fundraiser for Biden at his California home in coming weeks,[53] clearly thought it was within his bounds to offer policy advice to the president, whom he considered out of line for not supporting Amal's efforts to prosecute the government of Israel. There has been no further word out of the administration condemning the ICC. Congress did draft a bill to sanction the Court, potentially including Amal Clooney, but Biden signaled he did not support the legislation.[54] The fundraiser went on as planned, and reportedly raked in $30 million for Biden's reelection campaign,[55] although Clooney did subsequently implore Biden to withdraw from the race after the disastrous first debate in June.[56] The president officially quit the race the following month, making Harris the nominee.

In the media circus and political drama that followed, a curious event got largely overlooked. But on July 9, Director of National Intelligence Avril Haines released an official statement accusing Iran of supporting the pro-Hamas demonstrations in the United States that broke out after October 7, which Iran apparently considered an extension of the terrorist attacks it had sponsored.[57] Despite credible open-source reporting that Iranian officials had been actively part of the planning and execution of the Hamas attack, however, the Biden administration had been reluctant to point the finger at Tehran, possibly because they were still hoping for a return to the Obama-era nuclear deal.[58] Iranian-proxy attacks on American assets and commercial shipping in the region ratcheted up, including the killing of three U.S. servicemembers and wounding more than thirty others in Jordan in January.[59] Even after the direct attack from Iran on Israel in April, Biden tried to tamp down tensions, urging Netanyahu not to retaliate strongly.[60] So the official statement from the DNI stood out, indicating that the evidence of Iranian complicity in the American domestic demonstrations against Israel and for Hamas must be incontrovertible. For those paying attention, the episode chillingly demonstrated that for the Iranian regime, the attack on Israel and the destabilization in the United States were part of the same operation.

Postscript: The Vietnam Playbook Redux

As WE MARK THE first anniversary of October 7, 2023, the full picture of the war against Israel has taken form. The original terrorist attacks were only the beginning of the campaign to sever the United States from Israel and force the creation of a Palestinian entity while exposing a vulnerable and isolated Jewish state to international condemnation—or worse. Americans, writ large, may find it difficult to believe that Hamas's savage terrorist attacks could fuel a bid for statehood in the court of public opinion, but that is what is happening by design. Several Western countries, including Ireland, Norway, and Spain, have announced their recognition of a Palestinian state without any indication of what its borders might look like, and the Biden administration has signaled that the United States is open to the idea.[61]

In a haunting echo of the late 1960s on U.S. campuses, Hamas is currently achieving success in the United States that it cannot hope to win in Gaza—which is why an American needed to write this book. While it is about defending Israel, it is also about the role of this defense in preserving the United States from an ugly bigotry now manifest at home. Indeed, the campus radicals of our time were trained by those who fomented anti-war sentiment half a century ago. They have revived that Vietnam playbook of counterculture resistance to destroy the U.S.–Israel alliance and give terrorists an avenue to establish their state "from the river to the sea." As noted above, the Palestinians have actually lost every military engagement with Israel since 1967 but they have never been forced to accept this reality, so this remains their goal. If a president of the United States ever decides to acknowledge the actual truth and unequivocally declare Israel's victory, the sad history of U.S. engagement in Vietnam may not need to play out again in the Middle East.

Absent this clarity, Hamas—and its Iranian paymasters—may well be on their way to doing material damage to the Jewish state, and ultimately America. In the days after the rescue of the four Israeli hostages in Gaza, *The Wall Street Journal* published a long-form piece on the strategy of Yahya Sinwar, the leader of Hamas since 2017. It described how the terrorist mastermind willingly accepts civilian Palestinian casualties as a necessary sacrifice to further Hamas's goal to eradicate Israel. The article also reports that Sinwar's decision to start planning the October 7 attack happened three years earlier, during the 2021 Gaza war. For Sinwar, Israel's impressive missile defense against Hamas's rocket barrages, which was only going to get stronger, plus an appeasement-minded U.S. stance, equaled opportunity to shift tactics from projectiles to direct attacks.

Sinwar has also seen Hamas's fortunes change starting in January 2024, to the extent that he now believes Hamas "[has] the Israelis right where we want them." He has learned from past wars to use indiscriminate violence to break out of an intractable position and knows that if he controls the media he can do it with impunity and effectively demonize Israel in the press for fighting back.[62] He is now making progress towards recognition from the international community of a Palestinian state—and demonstrating significant support for this scheme on the streets of the United States.

CHAPTER TWO:
WHY ISRAEL?
AMERICA AND THE JEWISH STATE

The Dreyfus Affair

WHILE THE HOLOCAUST executed by Nazi Germany may be the most sensational example of antisemitism in Europe, hatred of Jews has been a perennial and insidious evil on the Continent since antiquity, gaining strength through the medieval period and persisting into our own time. Despised as an "inferior race," the Jews became Europe's routine outsider scapegoats. One of the most infamous instances of such scapegoating, the Dreyfus Affair in late-nineteenth-century France, was a harbinger of horrors to come—horrors that would necessitate the establishment of a Jewish state that would, in time, become a critical ally to the United States.

During the Third Republic, Alfred Dreyfus, a young Jewish army officer, was accused of selling military secrets to the Germans, including cutting-edge French weapon designs.[1] A document allegedly in Dreyfus's handwriting seemed to prove his guilt, and in January 1895 he was convicted of treason by a closed court martial. In a humiliating ceremony formally expelling him from the French army, Dreyfus's medals and insignia of rank were torn from his uniform and his sword broken, and he was paraded in front of the assembled officers, who jeered him as a traitor and a Jew. He was shipped off to Devil's Island, the notorious penal colony off the coast of French Guiana, where the mortality rate was so high that it was known as the "dry guillotine."

That should have been the end of Dreyfus, but the lack of substantial evidence remained troubling to some observers, as did the growing impression that he had been targeted primarily because he was a Jew. Eventually it was revealed that it would have been logistically impossible for Dreyfus to have had dealings with the Germans in question. Another suspect emerged, one whose handwriting more closely matched the incriminating document than Dreyfus's. The case that had once seemed open and shut began to look like a set-up.

The Dreyfus Affair was hotly debated between the traditionalists, who saw the controversy as a Jewish plot to undermine traditional French military culture, and progressives, who believed the persecution of Dreyfus was a shameful manifestation of antisemitism masked by the anti-German sentiment of that period following the Franco-Prussian War. The new French President Félix Faure, who had inherited the scandal, became the de facto leader of the traditionalists, while the journalist and future prime minister Georges Clemenceau spearheaded the effort to clear Dreyfus.

On January 13, 1898, the front page of Clemenceau's newspaper L'Aurore screamed "J'Accuse … !" Distilling the concerns and misgivings about the Dreyfus affair into one resonant phrase, the headline introduced an open letter to President Faure by the critic and author Émile Zola. It was the most detailed account of the injustices done to Dreyfus and a warning to the president that the scandal threatened to engulf his administration. Acknowledging that his letter potentially violated the law as libel, Zola defiantly declared, "My fiery protest is the cry of my very soul."[2]

Zola was duly convicted of libel and fled to England, but the case against Dreyfus began to fall apart. A second court martial convicted him again but commuted his sentence, and ten days later he was pardoned by a new president. Acceptance of the pardon required an admission of guilt, but Dreyfus was fully exonerated in 1906.

While justice had finally been done for Dreyfus, Jews sensed a growing threat. Many believed that they could no longer depend on assimilating into European culture, as had been the hope, but needed to establish their own state to protect themselves. The Dreyfus affair inspired the pioneering Zionist Theodor Herzl to write *The Jewish State: An Attempt at a Modern Solution to the Jewish Problem* in 1896, laying out the case for reestablishing a Jewish nation in the Holy Land.

The concept was hardly new, as Jews had been living in the region for millennia and had governed it as far back as the time of King David. But for the Austro-Hungarian Herzl, the pogroms of isolation and marginalization of the nineteenth century made the project immediate and urgent. As a young man he had hoped that enlightenment would lead to the end of antisemitism. However, he came to believe that hatred of Jews in Europe was so entrenched that the only real solution was a state for Jews in their ancestral homeland, where they could live and worship in peace and security. Herzl pressed his case with everyone from the Ottoman Sultan Abdul Hamid II to Kaiser Wilhelm II of Germany. The organizations that would eventually provide the foundation of the Israeli government, notably the Zionist Congress and the Jewish Agency, were formed.

Herzl's proposition was controversial, but it was also powerful, and modern Zionism gained steam after his death in 1904. Had his vision of a safe haven for Jews been realized in the early twentieth century, one of the greatest evils in history might have been avoided. But it was not yet to be. The gathering antisemitism he identified in European society spread into the mainstream in Germany in the 1920s, feeding on the general discontent following Germany's humiliating loss in World War I.

The Holocaust

WHILE ADOLF HITLER PERSONIFIES this movement, the Führer hardly came out of nowhere. The belief that Jews were at the root of Europe's problems was based on pseudoscience that justified their deportation, if not extermination, for the greater good. In this context, "science" was neither transparent nor neutral but was manipulated to support an extremist ideology.

For Hitler's Third Reich, which claimed descent from the medieval Holy Roman Empire, patriotism demanded the eradication of the stain of Judaism from culture and science. Jews represented an alien ethnic corruption that threatened the great Aryan nation and could not be

THE BATTLE FOR THE JEWISH STATE

tolerated. This concept held sway over German academia, where purges of Jewish scholars became common and the works of authors such as Sigmund Freud and Karl Marx were consigned to the flames. Special invective was reserved for the renowned physicist Albert Einstein of the Kaiser Wilhelm Institute in Berlin. Einstein had come to international prominence in 1905 when he published his Special Theory of Relativity, among four major achievements that year, on his way to his General Theory of Relativity published in 1915 and a Nobel Prize in physics in 1921. But Einstein was a Jew, and from a Nazi perspective this recognition of his achievements represented the corruption of real science.

Einstein's case illustrates the larger intellectual effort to justify antisemitism in Hitler's Germany. He was attacked by a pair of Nazi Nobel laureates, Philipp Lenard and Johannes Stark, who were determined to discredit Einstein as a scientist because he was a Jew.[3] He was a fraud, they charged, who had only repackaged the real science, which had been discovered by Aryans, Lenard and Stark among them. "Jewish physics," as they defined it, was subjective, convoluted, and abstract, while true science was the objective pursuit of truth. As Lenard put it, "It was precisely the yearning of Nordic man to investigate a hypothetical interconnectedness in nature which was the origin of natural science."

Einstein, fortunately, was able to escape via Great Britain to the United States before the Third Reich fully infiltrated German academia.[4] Many others were not so lucky. By 1941 Hitler's plan for ridding Germany of the Jews had progressed from deportation to annihilation.

What set Hitler apart was not his antisemitism; it was his ability to harness modern technology to facilitate mass murder on an unprecedented scale. During Operation Reinhard (1942–43), for example, some 25 percent of all the Jews killed during the Holocaust were murdered in a hundred-day unprecedented orgy of violence.[5] The method of choice was the gas chamber, which had been a rudimentary early nineteenth-century technology developed and made exponentially more efficient and lethal for the concentration camps of Dachau and Auschwitz. They were followed by death camps of Belzec, Chelmno, Sobibor, and

Treblinka, where larger gas chambers delivering the new cyanide poison Zyklon-B facilitated murder on an industrial scale. The camps were generally built close to railway lines to facilitate mass transport, in rural, wooded sites because the Nazis at least tried to hide their depravity until they achieved their goal.

At length, the United States entered the war after the Imperial Japanese attack on Pearl Harbor in 1941. Some Jewish refugees, such as Einstein, had found a home in America, but many more had been turned away to look for other safe havens or return to almost certain death in Europe. But the "greatest generation" rallied, and, under General Dwight D. Eisenhower, the Americans executed D-Day in 1944 and fought their way across Europe, finally defeating the Nazis and liberating those remaining in the camps.

The Nazis were prevented from completing their genocide by the collective response of the West, which was able to identify and eradicate their evil. The great lesson of the Holocaust should be that antisemitism is a noxious cancer that can corrupt and consume a great culture. It is tolerated and justified at our peril. We cannot assume that pledges of "never again" will effectively combat antisemitism. Each generation must confront it anew.

Ominously, in the years after Einstein arrived in the United States, he was disconcerted by the antisemitism he found already taking root in American academia. "The hostile attitude of universities towards Jewish teaching staff and students has been increasing perilously, even though it manifests in a hypocritical manner," Einstein wrote to his fellow physicist Paul Epstein in 1935. "Unfortunately, the current Jewish leaders do not comprehend the seriousness of the situation, similar to the German Jews in the time before Hitler. They believe that they are able to put an end to the problem by being silent and disregarding it, and they thus miss the time for creating places of support."[6]

Some six million of the nine million Jews living in Europe at the beginning of World War II were exterminated by the Third Reich. After the horrors of the Holocaust, it was impossible to deny that the Jews had to be able to protect themselves independently; a Jewish state in the Holy Land as Herzl envisioned was one logical way of how to do it. There were no remaining illusions that Europe could be a safe haven. Those who, since October 7, 2023, taunt Jews with "Go back to Poland" know, shamefully, exactly what going back might have entailed.

Israel and the Israelites

HOWEVER RIGHTEOUS THE CAUSE, establishing a sovereign Jewish state in the Holy Land was extraordinarily complicated. This strip of territory on the eastern Mediterranean coast had been contested by competing empires since antiquity, and the Muslim conquest in the seventh century, which eventually provoked the Christian Crusades of the twelfth and thirteenth centuries, left a legacy of turmoil.

But the Jewish roots in the region go far deeper than any other people's—three thousand years, in fact. While much of this tradition rests on the Biblical accounts ranging from Abraham, Moses, and David to Jesus of Nazareth, there is also voluminous evidence from other ancient texts and from modern archaeological excavations.[7]

The Israelites were delivered out of slavery in Egypt by the Old Testament hero Moses in the early thirteenth century B.C. Their invasion of Canaan, narrated by the Book of Joshua, took place around 1250 B.C., and they conquered Jerusalem under King David two centuries later. David's son Solomon built the First Temple on Mount Moriah. Completed in 957 B.C., it stood until the Babylonian invasion in the sixth century.

In 597 B.C., large numbers of Jews were enslaved by the Babylonians in Mesopotamia, where they languished until 539, when the Persian emperor Cyrus the Great conquered the Babylonians in their turn and made the extraordinary decision to release the Israelites. According to the Torah, Cyrus issued an edict after his conquest authorizing the liberation of Israelites enslaved by the Babylonians and the rebuilding of the Temple in Jerusalem. The Book of Isaiah says,

This is what the Lord says to his anointed, to Cyrus, whose right hand I take hold of to subdue nations before him and to strip kings of their armor, to open doors before him so that gates will not be shut: I will go before you and will level the mountains; I will break down gates of bronze and cut through bars of iron. I will give you hidden treasures, riches stored in secret places, so that you may know that I am the Lord, the God of Israel, who summons you by name.[8]

What was known in antiquity as the land of the Philistines, or Palestina, figures in numerous classical texts. The fifth-century B.C. Greek historian and geographer Herodotus, for example, writes of the eastern coast of the Mediterranean, "Now from the Persian country to Phoenicia there is a wide and vast tract of land; and from Phoenicia this peninsula runs beside our sea by way of the Syrian Palestine and Egypt, which is at the end of it; in this peninsula there are just three nations."[9]

The Romans generally referred to the area as the province of Judea, the land of the Jews. Originally, this territory was incorporated as a client kingdom into the emerging empire, famously ruled by King Herod the Great from 34 B.C. to A.D. 4. The most thorough literary treatment of Judea during the time of Jesus comes from the Roman historian Flavius Josephus's *Antiquities of the Jews*, including the *Wars of the Jews*. This volume treats in detail the decisive conquest of Jerusalem by the Emperors Vespasian and Titus in A.D. 70, including the destruction of the Second Temple and the siege of the Herodic fortress of Masada, where the Jewish defenders committed suicide rather than be taken captive by the Roman besiegers. These events ended Jewish rule of Judea but not the Jewish presence there, and it remained a province of the Eastern Roman Empire until the seventh century.

Nearly two thousand years of Jewish history predates the arrival of the Muslims, who seized Jerusalem from the Byzantines in A.D. 638, setting off centuries of strife between their caliphate and the Christian Crusaders who also laid claim to the Holy Land. The duration of the Jewish presence in Israel does not negate the undeniable Islamic or Christian heritage of the region, but it does put the lie to the narrative of the foundation of modern Israel as a European imposition on the indigenous people of the region, as is generally asserted by the proponents of Critical Race Theory.[10]

Ongoing archaeological excavations, begun by the British Palestine Exploration Fund in the nineteenth century, provide increasing physical evidence for Jewish rule of Israel during the period of the First Book of Kings. In the City of David archaeological park in Jerusalem, a series of significant finds over the past twenty years have established the location of King David's original palace at the foot of Mount Moriah outside the city's fortified walls, as well details of the First Temple period chronology.[11]

And critically, modern Israel was not exclusively the product of collective European guilt for the Holocaust after World War II. In fact, the existing Jewish population in the region had grown sporadically under the Ottoman Empire (1517–1922). A more coordinated wave of immigration took place in the First Aliya, or homecoming, which took place between 1881 and 1901. Driven by persecution in both Eastern Europe and the Middle East, some twenty-five thousand immigrants roughly doubled the Jewish population in the Holy Land. The Second Aliya (1904–14), launched after Herzl published *The Jewish State* in 1896, added another thirty-five thousand Jews, and the third (1919–23) added forty thousand.

By the end of World War I, the Jewish population in the Holy Land was thus growing rapidly, as were tensions with the Muslim population. The Great War had finally ended the decrepit Ottoman Empire, which had nominally governed the area until its defeat and dissolution. Great Britain delivered the coup de grâce, and in 1920 the British army was given a mandate to govern Palestine by the fledgling League of Nations,[12] which had been formed in the wake of the war in the hope—misplaced, as it turned out—of preventing such a conflict from breaking out again.

The British fight against the Ottomans had been supported by the Jewish Legion of more than one thousand volunteers, some of whom had come from America.[13] Organized by a Russian émigré named Vladimir (Ze'ev) Jabotinsky, they performed with distinction. Jabotinsky had become the leader of the Zionist movement in 1904 after Herzl's death, and was a passionate, if controversial, advocate for a Jewish state.

After being briefly imprisoned for his role in the 1920 riots in Jerusalem, Jabotinsky penned his groundbreaking essay, "The Iron Wall," in 1923. Presciently, he observed that until the Arabs were absolutely convinced there was no alternative to accepting the presence of Jews in the Holy Land, they would revert to their "Plan A," the eradication of the Jews, and there could be no reasonable negotiated "Plan B."[14]

Of course, Jabotinsky wrote in early twentieth-century terms that are highly contentious today; "colonialism" was not for him a dirty word. But old-fashioned rhetoric should not blind us to his keen insight into how to resolve the conflict between the Palestinians and the Jews, which Jabotinsky didn't believe was possible in 1923 but hoped could occur in the future. In the interim, he proposed an "iron wall" that would unfailingly protect Jews so that the Palestinians, even if they would not accept the Jews, would have to accept that they could not be eradicated.

If October 7 has taught us anything, it is that Jabotinsky was correct.

Israel and the United States

AFTER THE AXIS POWERS had been decisively defeated in World War II, the League of Nations' successor organization, the United Nations, turned its attention to how the Holy Land should be governed. The Balfour Declaration of 1917 stated Britain's intention to establish a Jewish state through the partition of the territory in Palestine that had been part of the Ottoman Empire, but there was no operational plan to implement it. There were about 1.2 million Arabs and six hundred thousand Jews living in the area, and there was little or no agreement about how the maps should be drawn or who should control Jerusalem. By 1939, British policy had shifted in favor of the Arabs in the wake of intermittent fighting between the two parties, and restrictions were placed on Jewish immigration to the region.

The British, exhausted from World War II and with no solution to these intractable problems, decided they needed to end their mandate.

The issue then moved to the United Nations, where the United States strongly supported the formation of the modern state of Israel. Despite opposition from Arab nations, on November 29, 1947, the United Nations adopted Resolution 181, approving the establishment of intertwined Arab and Jewish states, with Great Britain to retain control of the area during the months of transition.

Managing that transition for what would become Israel was an aspiring politician named David Ben-Gurion. Having arrived in the Holy Land from Poland as David Gruen in 1906, he later adopted an ancient Hebrew name. Like Jabotinsky, he had served in the British army in the First World War and participated in the liberation of Palestine from the Ottomans. He then set to work planning for the political independence of a Jewish state.

By July 1946, relations with the British forces in Jerusalem had deteriorated so badly that a Zionist paramilitary organization known as Irgun bombed the King David Hotel, the British headquarters in Jerusalem. Built of pink marble on a high point overlooking the Old City, the King David was one of Jerusalem's most prominent landmarks. Despite attempts to warn the British of the attack, ninety-one people were killed.

Having lost significant British support, Ben-Gurion turned his attention to the United States, a country he knew well. President Truman was a vocal advocate for a Jewish state, which enjoyed strong bipartisan support in both houses of Congress. In a foreshadowing of what would occur under subsequent Democrat administrations, the staunchly pro-Arabist Department of State, however, led by George Marshall, opposed recognition of Israel.[15]

The day the British mandate for Palestine expired, May 14, 1948, David Ben-Gurion declared the formation of the State of Israel, in accordance with United Nations General Assembly Resolution 181, with borders mapped out by the U.N.. As he made the announcement, gunfire could be heard in the background, and the next day the collective Arab world attacked.

Anticipating this course of events, Ben-Gurion had begun to organize the individual Jewish militias into a unified military. He was not only the first prime minister of Israel but also its first defense minister, recognizing that military matters were going to be the priority of the new government if it were to survive.

At President Truman's direction, the United States was the first country to recognize Israel as a sovereign nation, just eleven minutes after Ben-Gurion's announcement. Despite opposition within his own administration, the president went with his gut, approving a telegram that read:

> This Government has been informed that a Jewish state has been proclaimed in Palestine, and recognition has been requested by the provisional government thereof. The United States recognizes the provisional government as the de facto authority of the state of Israel.

Truman signed it personally.

This new partnership between the United States and Israel rested on a longstanding tradition of American sympathy for Judaism. George Washington, John Adams, and other founders, though Christian, admired and studied Judaism as they self-consciously formed a constitutional order based on Judeo-Christian values.[16] While this was not a uniform position, it was broadly held and influential.

During his first term as president, Washington visited the synagogue in Newport, Rhode Island—one of four synagogues then active in the United States—receiving a warm welcome from Rabbi Moses Seixas, who likened him to the Old Testament heroes David, Daniel, and Joshua.[17] Washington responded in a famous letter, declaring that tolerance was no longer an "indulgence" that one class of citizens granted to another but the natural right of all citizens, and concluding with the poetic benediction, "May the Children of the Stock of Abraham, who dwell in this land, continue to merit and enjoy the good will of the other Inhabitants; while every one shall sit in safety under his own vine and figtree, and there shall be none to make him afraid."[18]

Adams, who had grappled with the challenges of establishing a sovereign country in the North American colonies, took Washington's vision a step further and envisioned a Jewish state in Palestine decades before Herzl published *The Jewish State*. In 1818 he wrote to the prominent Rabbi Mordechai Manuel Noah regarding the latter's travels to Europe and Africa:

> I Should wish you had been a member of Napoleons Institute at Cairo nay farther I could find it in my heart to wish that you had been at the head of a hundred thousand Israelites indeed as well disciplin'd as a French army—& marching with them into Judea & making a conquest of that country & restoring your nation to the dominion of it—For I really wish the Jews again in Judea an independent nation For as I believe the most enlighten'd men of it have participated in the ameliorations of the philosophy of the age, once restored to an independent government & no longer persecuted they would soon wear away some of the asperities & peculiarities of their character possibly in time become liberal Unitarian Christians for your Jehovah is our Jehovah & your God of Abraham Isaac & Jacob is our God.[19]

Decades later, President-elect Abraham Lincoln would refer to himself as the inheritor of the revolutionary struggle to establish the United States in Biblical terms invoking the Jewish people, as a "humble instrument in the hands of the Almighty, and of this, his almost chosen people, for perpetuating the object of that great struggle."[20]

While making up less than 1 percent of the American population in 1776, Jews and Judaism had a prominent role in the founding of the United States and its institutions. Of course, the past 275 years have not been uniformly idyllic for American Jews, who have encountered antisemitism in the United States as they have around the globe. In 1982, for example, when Israel's war in southern Lebanon sparked an outbreak of antisemitism, the author Norman Podhoretz revived Zola's renowned headline "J'Accuse..." to expose a Jew-hatred that was eerily similar to what we are seeing again today.[21]

Nevertheless, the biblical values on which our civilization rests have always promoted an alliance between Christians and Jews, ensuring that Jews were a vital part of the American experiment throughout our history. The progressive rejection of "Judeo-Christian values" in recent years, however, threatens both the legacy of our greatest American leaders and our alliance with the state of Israel. But as has been exposed since October 7, in the academic context of Critical Race Theory, the once-uncontroversial statement that the United States was founded on Judeo-Christian values, which were then echoed in the founding of Israel and form the basis for our lasting alliance, has become a rallying cry to attack both the founding fathers and Israel. In CRT-speak, rather than "Judeo-Christian values" being evidence of tolerance, they have become harbingers of racism—if as values they even exist at all.[22]

The History of the U.S–Israel Security Partnership

WHILE THE U.S.–ISRAEL ALLIANCE has its roots in the Judeo-Christian moral tradition that informed the founding of both countries, as the relationship has matured, shared interests have given this partnership a practical dimension as well. The prospect of an Arab attack on Israel at the time of the foundation of the Jewish state made it clear that external military assistance was necessary from the start. The United States was not always the primary supporter of Israel, which originally had closer security relations with the Soviets and later with France. But the U.S.-Israel partnership developed over time, and while America has naturally been the "big brother," the relationship has matured to the benefit of both countries.

From Herzl's time, establishing a physical safe haven for Jews to protect them from violent antisemitism defined the Zionist project. Both Jabotinsky and Ben-Gurion had focused on establishing a powerful Jewish military that could deter or, if necessary, defeat any enemy. Jabotinsky is reported to have declared, "It is better to own a gun and not need it than to not own a gun and need it."

Ben-Gurion and Jabotinsky were joined in this effort by the man who would become Israel's first president, Chaim Weizmann. Although less well-known now, Weizmann played a critical role in the establishment of Israel, as well as in developing the U.S.–Israel alliance.

Born in Russia, Weizmann became a pioneering chemist at the University of Manchester, and during World War I invented a process that facilitated the production of synthetic acetone, critical to manufacturing ammunition, for which the Allies had previously been dependent on Germany. He became increasingly committed to the Zionist goal of establishing a Jewish state and through his friendship with Arthur, Lord Balfour, the British foreign secretary, helped craft the Balfour Declaration, expressing Britain's intent to establish a Jewish homeland in Palestine. Weizmann then went to America, where he facilitated Albert Einstein's first visit in 1921 to raise funds for a new Hebrew University in Jerusalem.[23] He immigrated to Palestine in the 1930s and attempted to evacuate European Jews to the Holy Land before World War II broke out.

When Ben-Gurion became Israel's first prime minister, Weizmann, the head of the Israel's premier scientific research institution, the Weizmann Institute, became the first president. While his contributions to Israel are innumerable, Weizmann's key legacy was to establish the link between the ingenuity of Israel's people and the defense of the Jewish state.

The first Arab–Israeli War—also called the War of Independence—raged from May 15, 1948, the day after Israel was founded while the British forces withdrew, to March 10, 1949. The Arab Liberation Army—comprising forces from Lebanon (then known as Transjordan), Egypt, and Iraq—attempted to overwhelm the fledgling nation in what ought to have been a bloodbath. U.S. Secretary of Defense James Forrestal, who along with his State Department colleagues had opposed U.S. recognition of Israel, pointed out that there were some thirty million Arabs in the region and only about six hundred thousand Jews.[24] It seemed a losing proposition. But Israel fought back.

Israel's new government had closely tracked attempts by the Arabs to cut off vital supply chains in the days before the declaration of statehood and focused on retaining these channels of access, as well as securing the necessary territory to protect them. After some initial setbacks, Ben-Gurion was able to unify the various paramilitary forces that had been fighting independently into a single force that would become the Israel Defense Forces (IDF) and to obtain desperately needed recruits and supplies from abroad. In July, Israeli forces started to defeat the Arabs and take back territory. By the end of the year the fighting was largely over, and Israel was intact.

While some volunteers came from America, no military supplies were offered, and the United States maintained an arms embargo on both sides. President Truman supported Israel, but he faced a hotly contested election in 1948, and the country had no appetite for involvement in another foreign war. Truman, then Eisenhower after him, also knew there would be challenges in southeast Asia as America recovered from World War II.

Israel, however, was able to prevail largely on its own in the War of Independence. By the spring of 1949 it was negotiating armistice agreements with the Arab states that had attacked and establishing a new and more defensible map for the Jewish state. The Palestinians, however, refused to come to terms with Israel, and a tenuous, uneasy status quo prevailed until 1956.

The United States did not support Israel in the war that broke out that year between Israel and Egypt. The Suez Crisis saw the Jewish state joined by Great Britain and France in an effort to end the Egyptian blockade of the Suez Canal. In fact, President Dwight Eisenhower exerted substantial pressure on Prime Minister Ben-Gurion to withdraw from territory in the Sinai Peninsula that Israel had taken during the conflict. In his desire for Ben-Gurion to defer to the United Nations, Eisenhower set the stage for generations of futile efforts to trade Israeli territory for peace with its Arab neighbors.[25]

In the months before the Suez Crisis, some combination of Egyptian soldiers and Palestinians attacked a kibbutz, or agricultural community, in southern Israel near Gaza. A young Israeli guard, Roi Rotberg, was killed, and his eulogy was given by one of the IDF's greatest generals, Moshe Dayan.

Dayan had been born in 1915 in what is now Syria and had participated in the foundation of Israel before playing a critical role in the wars that followed, losing an eye fighting in 1941 and adopting his signature black eye patch. Given the disparity in populations between the Arabs and Jews, he believed fiercely that each time the Arabs attacked, the Jews had to respond ever more forcefully to establish deterrence, and that no Israeli could for a moment forget the threat under which they lived. For Roi, Dayan said, the problem was that because he lived in peace, he assumed others would as well—which turned out to be a deadly assumption:

The millions of Jews, annihilated without a land, peer out at us from the ashes of Israeli history and command us to settle and rebuild a land for our people. But beyond the furrow that marks the border, lies a surging sea of hatred and vengeance, yearning for the day that the tranquility blunts our alertness, for the day that we heed the ambassadors of conspiring hypocrisy, who call for us to lay down our arms.

It is to us that the blood of Roi calls from his shredded body. Although we have vowed a thousand vows that our blood will never again be shed in vain—yesterday we were once again seduced, brought to listen, to believe. Our reckoning with ourselves, we shall make today. We mustn't flinch from the hatred that accompanies and fills the lives of hundreds of thousands of Arabs, who live around us and are waiting for the moment when their hands may claim our blood. We mustn't avert our eyes, lest our hands be weakened. That is the decree of our generation. That is the choice of our lives—to be willing and armed, strong and unyielding, lest the sword be knocked from our fists, and our lives severed.

Roi Rotberg, the thin blond lad who left Tel Aviv in order to build his home alongside the gates of Gaza, to serve as our wall. Roi—the light in his heart blinded his eyes and he saw not the flash of the blade. The longing for peace deafened his ears and he heard not the sound of the coiled murderers. The gates of Gaza were too heavy for his shoulders, and they crushed him.[26]

Like Jabotinsky before him in his analysis of the fraught Israel–Palestinian dynamic, particularly in terms of Gaza, Dayan was all too grimly prophetic.

Within a decade of the 1956 war, however, the position of the United States began to shift because of growing pressures from the Cold War. The Soviets, allies during World War II, had participated in the liberation of the Nazi death camps and had generally supported the establishment of Israel. Ben-Gurion had even tried to find common ground with the Soviet Union's permanent representative to the United Nations, Andrei Gromyko, in 1947 by emphasizing Zionism's adherence to socialism.[27] After all, some of Dreyfus's staunchest supporters in nineteenth-century France had been communists. But the Soviets eventually allied themselves with the Arabs, supplying Israel's enemies with increasingly sophisticated weapons that could overwhelm the Jewish state. Seeing Zionism as an imperialist Western plot to expand U.S. influence, Moscow also ratcheted up its persecution of Russian Jews.

Concerned about Soviet domination of the Middle East and its increasingly vital energy resources, President Lyndon Johnson started to change U.S. policy toward military support for Israel. Until then, America had provided Israel with only limited defensive weapons. Johnson approved sales of tanks and aircraft in 1965, hoping to deter the Arabs from engaging in an arms race that would lead to another war.[28]

Johnson's policy shift was not decisive, however, and the United States once again played an equivocal role, this time in the Six-Day War of 1967. U.S.–Israel relations were complicated by the Israeli attack on USS *Liberty* off the Sinai Peninsula, which killed some three dozen Americans and injured 171. Israel insisted the incident was a case of mistaken identity, an explanation the U.S. government accepted but that many Americans have disputed. Whatever might have been the truth behind the *Liberty* incident, the partnership between Israel and the United States remained far from seamless.

As in 1948 and 1956, Israel achieved a swift military victory in the Six-Day War over what should have been a more powerful adversary—in this case, the combined forces of Egypt, Syria, and Jordan. Defeating all three countries under Dayan's brilliant leadership, Israel seized not only the Sinai but also Gaza, the West Bank, and the Golan Heights, all of which had been used to launch Palestinian terrorist attacks on the Jewish state.

In hindsight, it seems that 1967 should have been an opportunity to declare Israel's victory and force the Palestinians to realize that they and the Arab nations supporting them had decisively lost three successive wars. Truly secure borders for Israel might have been established and the future of the Palestinian refugees, to be settled in a demilitarized territory, resolved.

Instead, the United Nations and the Johnson administration once again urged Israel to exercise "restraint" and to accept the two-state formula that had been the basis of the original Balfour Declaration. The U.N. Security Council adopted UNSCR 242, once again calling on Israel to trade territory for peace. The resolution proposed that Israel return the land it had seized in the war in return for "[t]ermination of all states of belligerency and respect for and acknowledgement of the sovereignty, territorial integrity and political independence of every State in the area and their right to live in peace within secure and recognized boundaries free from threats or acts of force."[29]

Egypt, Jordan, and Syria, eager to get their territory back in exchange for an abstract promise of peace, accepted the resolution. The recently formed Palestine Liberation Organization (PLO), however, did not, as its charter called for a single Palestinian state that would entirely eliminate Israel. But UNSCR 242 became the default basis for future negotiations to resolve the Israel–Palestinian conflict, on the assumption that an enduring peace deal would be based on the 1967 borders that allowed for the return of refugees. Yet the very reason the Six-Day War had been fought was that the 1967 borders were not defensible for Israel, inevitably exposing its people to deadly vulnerability. Furthermore, the United Nations' definition of Palestinian refugees, as both the originally displaced persons along with all their descendants, was incompatible with Israel's Jewish identity, dooming these efforts to failure.

Despite the Johnson administration's tepid response to Israel's astonishing success in 1967, it was now apparent that the Israel Defense Forces could be a unique and eminently capable security partner for the United States in the Middle East—and the United States needed partners. The war in Vietnam was not going well, and opposition at home was spreading. The Viet Cong's willing stooges in the media and entertainment, from Walter Cronkite[30] to Jane Fonda, suggested that not only was the United States losing the war, but that it was also on the wrong side altogether. America's choices, they insisted, were to cut and run or to side with the romantically revolutionary "freedom fighters" (and turn a blind eye to the savage human rights abuses and oppression of the communist North Vietnamese). Fonda went so far as to visit North Vietnam and pose for photographs in a helmet with Viet Cong fighters, earning herself the nickname "Hanoi Jane." In her later years the actress had regret for her actions—but the damage was done at the time.[31]

Americans were on edge as the assassinations of Martin Luther King Jr. and Robert F. Kennedy set off violent riots in cities and on campuses, compounding the general sense that the country was out of control and increasing opposition to the effort in Vietnam. Johnson had become so unpopular during the war that he declined to run for reelection in 1968, and Richard Nixon won the presidency. College anti-war protests became increasingly violent, most infamously at Kent State University in Ohio, where four students were killed in 1970. Regardless of how the war was going on the battlefield, it was being lost in America.

Nixon's twin priorities when he assumed office were to end the war in Vietnam and manage the Cold War, two enormous preoccupations that might have overshadowed Israel. But Nixon, whose occasional antisemitic remarks were later revealed by his secretly recorded Oval Office tapes, appointed Henry Kissinger as his national security advisor (later double-hatting him as secretary of state), making him one of the most powerful Jews in the history of the U.S. government. In 1973, the two of them may well have saved Israel.

On Yom Kippur of that year, the holiest day of the Jewish calendar, Egypt and Syria launched a surprise joint attack on Israel. Efforts had been made to build up the IDF's arsenal in the years since the Six-Day War, but Egypt and Syria were now being supplied by the Soviets, and the forces arrayed against the Jewish state dwarfed anything Israel could muster. In the north, 180 Israeli tanks would have to defend against 400 Syrian tanks, while in the south more than eighty thousand Egyptian soldiers prepared to attack just 436 members of the IDF.[32] Nixon, who saw the conflict through the prism of the Cold War, understood that if Israel failed, the Soviets would be the dominant power in the Middle East.

The prime minister of Israel, Golda Meir, sent a distress signal to Washington. Born in Kiev but raised in the United States, she had immigrated to Ottoman Palestine in 1921 and was elected to the Knesset in Israel's earliest days. She served as labor minister and then foreign minister to Prime Minister Ben-Gurion, becoming prime minister herself in 1969. She visited Washington that year and developed a cordial relationship with Nixon despite concerns in Washington about Israel's developing nuclear program.[33]

Nixon's response was decisive: Israel would not fail because its victory was in the critical national-security interest of the United States. At first, the Egyptians and Syrians made some advances into Israeli territory, but as the IDF regrouped, Nixon initiated Operation Nickel Glass, an unprecedented effort to resupply Israel by both air and sea. Nickel Glass gave the IDF the flexibility to expend munitions much more aggressively than it otherwise could have done, and perhaps more importantly, the unambiguous and sustained U.S. support bolstered Israel's confidence and rebutted the Arabs' assertion that the Jewish state was isolated.

To the amazement of all, especially the Arabs, Israel turned the tide. When it became clear that Egypt and Syria, despite Soviet backing, were going to lose the war they had started, they agreed to a ceasefire, and Israel retained the territory it had gained in 1967. Nixon, a Republican, made good on what Truman, a Democrat, had promised, establishing the United States as Israel's critical ally. Israel, for its part, had demonstrated an uncontested military dominance in the Middle East.

The year 1973 saw the end of formal military action by regional nation-states against Israel for half a century, during which time the U.S.–Israel partnership developed and matured regardless of who was president or prime minister. Benefitting from an unprecedented U.S. investment in its defenses, Israel became the largest single recipient of American military aid—more than $150 billion since 1948.[34] But unlike most foreign aid, which is framed as disinterested charity, this money has been an investment by American taxpayers in the security of both countries, bearing dividends for the American and the Israeli people.

The United States also emerged as Israel's diplomatic partner of choice. Under President Jimmy Carter, for example, Prime Minister Menachim Begin and Egyptian President Anwar Sadat concluded the first formal peace treaty between Israel and an Arab country. Begin and Sadat were an unlikely pair to make peace. The Russian-born Begin had been part of the Irgun force that executed the attack on the King David Hotel. Sadat, who had been Egyptian President Gamal Abdel Nasser's final vice president, succeeded to the presidency in 1970 after Nasser's death, and so oversaw the Yom Kippur attack on Israel.

Begin had not been close to Ben-Gurion and was a founder in the early 1970s of the Likud ("Consolidation") Party, which represented more conservative elements opposed to the then-dominant Labor Party. Likud enjoyed a landslide victory in the parliamentary elections of 1977, making Begin prime minister.

Sadat, like Nasser, came up through the powerful Egyptian military, but despite Egypt's close ties with the Soviet Union, he had an affinity for the United States, even training for a time with the U.S. Army in

America. Frustrated with the attempts to find a pan-Arab agreement with Israel, Sadat made the stunning announcement in November 1977 that he would be willing to go to Jerusalem and negotiate a peace treaty directly with the Israelis.

President Carter, a Democrat, had been blindsided by Likud's victory and assumed Begin would be a hardliner unwilling to make any concessions in peace talks. But Begin also saw the opportunity in Sadat's offer and engaged in more than a year of contentious negotiations, including the two-week marathon session in September 1978, known as the Camp David Accords.[35]

Finally, in March 1979, a deal was completed that would end the war between the two countries and establish diplomatic relations between them.[36] Israel would withdraw from the Sinai and offer certain unilateral concessions to the Palestinians. The Egyptians would guarantee Israel freedom of navigation through the Red Sea and the Suez Canal. For its part, the United States would guarantee the free flow of energy to Israel, which at that time was entirely dependent on energy imports. Begin and Sadat received the 1978 Nobel Peace Prize.

Carter successfully brokered the deal, establishing the indispensable role for the United States in negotiating bilateral agreements between Israel and its Arab neighbors, but at considerable cost. The president's myopic focus on securing this agreement blinded him to two momentous national security challenges for the United States in 1979, namely the Islamic revolution in Iran and the Soviet invasion of Afghanistan. Both events would have long-term consequences for American and Israeli security. Carter's inability to forestall or manage them contributed to the failures that cost him reelection in 1980.

Like Nixon before him, America's new president, Ronald Reagan, saw international affairs primarily through the prism of the Cold War. But unlike Nixon, whose approach to the Soviets—known as détente, or relaxation—sought to lower tensions and avoid confrontation, Reagan offered a simple but radical formula: We win, they lose.

In Reagan's view, Israel was the critical U.S. partner in the Middle East, especially after the American-allied shah of Iran was deposed in 1979. He pushed back against attempts to isolate Israel in international organizations, for example an Arab initiative to expel Israel from the United Nations. Speaking to a Jewish audience in Maryland in 1983, Reagan declared, "If Israel is ever forced to leave the United Nations, the United States and Israel will leave together."[37] Given his focus on winning the Cold War, however, relations with Israel were sometimes subordinated to other priorities. But while some of Reagan's policies could be seen as less favorable to Israel than others, many important security milestones during his administration led to the close cooperation the United States and Israel enjoy today.

The first was the establishment of the United States' formal commitment to calibrate arms sales to the rest of the Middle East to maintain Israel's qualitative military edge (QME) over its neighbors, a policy that Secretary of State Alexander Haig explicitly recognized in 1981.[38] The term refers to the calibration American war planners applied in anticipating a conflict with the Soviet Union in Europe. The Soviets would inevitably enjoy a vast advantage in the numbers of troops it could field, so the United States and NATO needed to have a counterbalancing advantage in the lethality and sophistication of the weapons they could deploy.

Reagan did have some challenges maintaining the QME with other commitments in the region, notably with the Saudis. Shortly after taking office, he announced an arms-sales package to the Kingdom that included five Airborne Warning and Control Systems (AWACS). AWACS are highly sophisticated plane-based radar systems, which essentially function as an early warning system. Israel was deeply concerned about this technology transfer as it had been developing its own version, the Airborne Early Warning & Control (AEW&C), after being surprised by invasion in both the Six-Day and Yom Kippur wars, which it wanted to remain supreme in the region.

The America Israel Public Affairs Committee (AIPAC), a powerful lobbying group, led the charge to organize opposition to the sale in Congress, and in the ensuing controversary the Reagan administration entered into negotiations with Israel to review the plan.[39] The result, in November 1981, was the first in the long series of Memoranda of Understanding (MOU) between the two countries.

The MOU laid out the parameters of a projected formal program of U.S.–Israel security cooperation in the context of the Cold War:

> United States-Israel strategic cooperation, as set forth in this memorandum, is designed against the threat to peace and security of the region caused by the Soviet Union or Soviet-controlled forces from outside the region introduced into the region. It has the following broad purposes:
>
> A. To enable the parties to act cooperatively and in a timely manner to deal with the above-mentioned threat.
>
> B. To provide each other with military assistance for operations of their forces in the area that may be required to cope with this threat.
>
> C. The strategic cooperation between the parties is not directed at any state or group of states within the region. It is intended solely for defensive purposes against the above-mentioned threat.[40]

By making the American commitment to Israel's QME explicit in an official document, the Reagan administration confirmed that the United States would not allow the Jewish state to be overwhelmed by the arms supplied to the Arabs by the Soviets. The Reagan administration also granted Israel major non-NATO-member ally status in 1987, opening the door to increased weapons sales and joint systems development.

The second Reagan-era milestone was in the intelligence field. As 1973 so painfully demonstrated—and October 7 would do in its turn—Israel could live or die by the quality of the information at its disposal. A priority of every Israeli prime minister starting with Ben-Gurion, therefore, was to achieve intelligence capabilities of the highest order.

The first agreement to expand intelligence cooperation and sharing between the United States and Israel had been signed in 1963, but in 1982

Reagan decided to codify and expand it as an official General Security of Information Agreement.[41] The bilateral intelligence relationship has grown in the subsequent decades, and while open-source accounts of this activity are understandably and rightly quite limited, the Reagan administration's initiative formed the bedrock of this critical cooperation that keeps Americans and Israelis safe.

Reagan's greatest contribution to the alliance, however, might at first seem to have nothing in particular to do with Israel. In a historic speech from the Oval Office in 1984, he announced the Strategic Defense Initiative (SDI),[42] a missile-defense program designed to neutralize Soviet intercontinental ballistic missiles before they could reach American or European soil. Rather than trying to make an offensive nuclear exchange so painful as to deter it, as had been the case under the "mutually assured destruction" scenario, Reagan's objective was to make launching nuclear-armed missiles futile. The president posed a simple question: "Wouldn't it be better to prevent deaths than to avenge them?"

Backlash from the Democrats to this ambitious—and expensive—initiative was swift and scathing. Senator Edward Kennedy mockingly nicknamed the project "Star Wars." Senator Joseph Biden was openly disdainful of Reagan's approach to the Cold War, which he considered reckless and provocative. In a 1986 speech to the National Press Club, Biden lambasted both SDI and Reagan: "Star Wars represents a fundamental assault on the concepts, alliances, and arms-control agreements that have buttressed American security for several decades, and the president's continued adherence to it constitutes one of the most reckless and irresponsible acts in the history of modern statecraft."[43]

While the concept of SDI was derided as the equivalent of "a bullet hitting a bullet,"[44] it turned out to be a viable deterrent to the Soviets and contributed to the bankrupting arms race that Reagan used to win the Cold War. And as Israel shifted from focusing on nation-state wars with Arab countries to coping with increasingly lethal terrorist rocket attacks from the Palestine Liberation Organization and other terrorist groups, SDI seemed like a divine inspiration.

Building the Iron Dome

REAGAN'S RATIONALE FOR LAUNCHING SDI in his 1983 speech could have been written by any Israeli Prime Minister: "I've become more and more deeply convinced that the human spirit must be capable of rising above dealing with other nations and human beings by threatening their existence. Feeling this way, I believe we must thoroughly examine every opportunity for reducing tensions and for introducing greater stability into the strategic calculus on both sides."

The year after Reagan announced SDI, the United States and Israel signed another MOU regarding missile defense cooperation.[45] Given Israel's location and threat profile, any such defensive capability was going to be tremendously appealing to the IDF. This MOU initiated an extraordinary period of joint research and development that was of great benefit to both countries. Philosophically, the inherently defensive nature of the endeavor was perfectly aligned with the strategy of both the United States and Israel. The trick was how to make it work.

The good news is that the systems that were developed through this cooperation over some four decades do indeed work. The bad news is that they have had to—some for the first time in the attacks on Israel that followed October 7.

The most famous component of the multilayered missile defense system that has been developed for Israel is the Iron Dome. Named in honor of Jabotinsky's impenetrable "Iron Wall," this mobile system protects against the kind of short- and medium-range projectiles that are typically used by the Iranian proxy groups Hezbollah and Hamas, both of which emerged as deadly threats to Israel and the United States in the 1980s.

The radical Shi'a Islamist Hezbollah, based in Lebanon, was formed during the long and torturous Lebanese civil war, which coincided with the revolution in Iran. In 1982, after the PLO launched a series of attacks on northern Israel from Lebanese territory, the IDF launched Operation Peace for Galilee.[46] This invasion of southern Lebanon played out against an increasingly violent series of terrorist attacks on U.S. interests in Beirut, culminating in the October 23, 1983 bombing of the Marine barracks, which took the lives of 241 servicemen in what was then the worst terrorist attack in history against Americans.[47] As intended, the attacks shook U.S. support for the Israeli invasion as the Reagan administration tried to chart a way out of an intractable situation.

The radical Sunni Islamist Hamas, which has murky origins in the Egyptian Muslim Brotherhood, is based in Gaza and carried out its first significant attack on Israel in 1989 when it abducted and murdered two Israeli soldiers. Hamas's attacks quickly escalated, fueled by arms flowing into the Strip from Egypt and its growing partnership with Hezbollah, which shared the goal of eradicating Israel.

It might seem incongruous for Sunni and Shi'a terrorist organizations to be making common cause, and Hezbollah and Hamas do have different priorities as well as interpretations of Islam. Hezbollah focuses on weakening Israel by projecting Iranian power on its borders as well as by carrying out international terrorist attacks on Iran's behalf, while Hamas's purpose is to directly destroy Israel and replace it with a Palestinian state. But they had two powerful motives to coordinate: their hatred for both the United States and Israel, and their mutual patronage by the new regime in Tehran. Through its Islamic Revolutionary Guard Corps (IRGC), the Iranian military funneled increasingly sophisticated weapons to both groups, while their intelligence services and even diplomatic corps provided information and financial support.

Over time, both Hezbollah and Hamas developed political as well as paramilitary elements and burrowed into all aspects of Lebanese and Gazan civil society, expanding both their resources and their power base. Hezbollah has had an elected presence in the Lebanese parliament for years and even held the majority from 2018 to 2022. As we have seen, Hamas won the local elections in Gaza in 2006, part of the George W. Bush administration's attempt to democratize the Middle East and has governed the strip ever since.

Hezbollah and Hamas are both designated Foreign Terrorist Organizations (FTO) by the United States. They deal regularly in abductions, torture, and assassinations, but they have recently used missile attacks on Israel to spread terror on a larger scale. During the Second Intifada, or "uprising," which began in 2001, Hamas indiscriminately fired rockets at civilian areas, hoping to inflict maximum casualties on soft targets.[48]

In 2006, Hezbollah fired rockets into northern Israel that hit the Jezreel Valley, close to the house of Chanoch Levin. Born in Tel Aviv in 1948, the year of Israel's founding, Levin was an engineer for Rafael, one of Israel's largest defense companies. After this harrowing experience, he went to his senior leadership with some ideas of how Rafael might develop a system to neutralize the projectiles before they struck. Levin later recalled the general skepticism that greeted his proposal:

> What were the difficulties at the start of the Iron Dome project? There was not a single person or group who did not oppose it. The entire defense establishment: chief of staff, the defense minister, many senior officers all claimed it is a fantasy, it cannot be done. A waste of money. I'll let you in on a secret. At the beginning, I also thought it was impossible. But we had to do it![49]

With a small team and modest budget, Levin went to work. Despite all the misgivings, they developed an autonomized system of an interceptor known as Tamir, software and radar that could identify a missile and trace its trajectory to gauge if it might hit a populated area. If so, an IDF monitor could fire the interceptor to destroy it. It was something of a pick-up game, with parts taken from electronic toys, as well as from Israel's most sophisticated technology producers. To make it mobile, Levin copied the design of the transport from industrial garbage trucks with their hydraulic lifts. This system became Iron Dome.

The United States was briefed on Iron Dome's progress, but it was developed exclusively with Israeli resources, making it proprietary intellectual property. The first successful test of the system was in 2009, and it was deployed in the field in 2011. Going from conception to deployment in only five years, Iron Dome was the embodiment of necessity being the mother of invention.

The successful system also embodied President Reagan's vision of saving lives instead of avenging them—on both sides of the conflict. As Iron Dome was being developed, Levin informed the Knesset that preventing Hamas's missiles from striking Israeli targets would alleviate the pressure on the IDF to invade Gaza to destroy the missiles before they were fired. Hamas's predilection for shielding their weapons with Palestinian citizens guaranteed disproportionate civilian casualties should such invasions be necessary.

The Iron Dome "Tamir" interceptors were designed to leave a prominent smoke trail behind them as they pursued their targets, giving the system a strange aerial beauty. In 2012 when the system was activated to neutralize a barrage of rockets launched towards Beersheba, rather than scattering to bomb shelters the revelers at a local wedding continued to dance under the flashes of the interceptions as if they were fireworks.[50]

The Iron Dome became the darling of the U.S. Congress, which started pouring resources into the program in 2011, and an agreement for technology sharing was signed in 2014.[51] The system was followed by joint programs between Rafael and the U.S. defense contractor Raytheon to protect against longer-range missiles, such as David's Sling and Arrow 2 & 3. An additional system, Arrow 4, is now in development.[52] While the U.S. Army has purchased some Iron Dome interceptors, there are problems with interoperability because the system was developed independently. Systems recently developed jointly by the United States and Israel should not have such problems.

The reliable protection provided by this multilayered missile-defense system may, in some ways, have made Israel the victim of its own success. When Hamas fired more than two thousand rockets at Israel during the eleven-day Gaza war in 2021, for example, Iron Dome had a more than 90 percent success rate intercepting them,[53] with press photographs capturing the gracefully spiraling interceptors destroying the rockets.[54] The Biden administration quickly demanded a ceasefire, and the Israeli government complied, judging that its reliable defenses made an incursion into Gaza unnecessary. In hindsight, that was the moment when Hamas's leader Yahya Sinwar, realizing that the Iron Dome had rendered its missiles and rockets largely useless, started planning for a very different sort of attack on Israel.

Beyond Security: Innovation and the "Start-Up Nation"

WHILE THE U.S.–ISRAEL SECURITY partnership has been the bedrock of the alliance since 1973, another aspect of the relationship, which has emerged since the turn of this century, has deepened and enriched it beyond military cooperation. Iron Dome represents the larger wave of extraordinary innovation that has fueled Israel's development from a poor and vulnerable nation reliant on economic support from the United States to a regional—indeed a global—economic and technological powerhouse.

The ingenuity and resourcefulness that have been hallmarks of modern Israel from its founding were originally focused on military applications, as the tiny country had to rely on a technological edge to offset its adversaries' advantages in population and resources. Chaim Weizmann's scientific genius, recognized by everyone from Franklin Roosevelt to Winston Churchill, was one of the foundation blocks of Israel. Lieutenant Uziel Gal of the IDF introduced the world to the Uzi submachine gun in 1952,[55] and innovations in missile defense, including Iron Dome, should be credited with helping to preserve the country.

The early years were not particularly promising for private-sector development, however. Israel's perpetually wartime economy, further strained by the need to support immigrants, had little breathing room for growth, was mainly focused on agriculture, and was heavily socialist. But these conditions began to change in the 1970s, when elements of the Likud party began to push back against the legacy of government controls and economic subsidies. The path from socialism to the so-called "start-up nation" was not smooth nor is it entirely complete, but there is no question that Israel has emerged as one of the most power-ful incubators of innovation on the planet. As such, Israel has become an indispensable economic partner to the United States, which is also increasingly reliant on maintaining technological advantages over com-petitors who are eager to steal and exploit intellectual property, notably the People's Republic of China.

Israel was the beneficiary of America's first Free Trade Agreement (FTA). Signed during the Reagan administration in 1985, the FTA has fostered increasing trade and cooperation in critical sectors such as civil aviation, space, health, energy, and agriculture.[56] Spurred by this scien-tific and technological cooperation, Israel emerged as a leader in the "dot-com" internet boom of the 1990s. Israel has the most start-up com-panies on the planet and is among the leaders in patents per capita. The Economic Support Funds (ESF), financial aid from the United States that had been vital to Israel's early survival, were no longer needed by the turn of the millennium, and the vast majority of the assistance now provided by America is invested in the defense partnership that benefits both countries.

Israelis have won an extraordinary thirteen Nobel prizes including four in chemistry and three in physics over the last fifty years, research that has been an enormous benefit not only to the Jewish state but to all humanity. Israel's track record on invention is so formidable that advo-cates for the pro-Palestinian "boycott, divest, and sanction" movement to isolate Israel economically are frequently befuddled by the difficulty of decoupling from Israeli tech. Just a few examples: Israel's Anobit has contributed critical components to iPhones for more than a decade.[57] Israeli scientists from Hebrew University developed the cherry tomato.[58] The pioneering navigation app Waze, developed in Israel, was purchased by Google in 2015.[59] In other words, this illustrious list shows it is now challenging to communicate, eat, or go anywhere without using Israeli technology, which is increasingly integrated into American technology.

Israel's economic expansion, especially after Benjamin Netanyahu's term as finance minister (2003–05) has been remarkable. Gross domestic product per capita rose from $27,500 in 2009 to $49,500 in 2023, and Israel was eleventh in the *U.S. News and World Report* annual ranking of influential countries that same year.[60] And all this success was based not on the traditional factors of resources and market size but rather on the power of innovation.

These achievements have not been unnoticed on the world stage, and even countries that have traditionally supported the Palestinian cause have also started to take a practical interest in Israel. Some Arab nations that have faced legal impediments to economic and technological cooperation due to the Arab Boycott are working to reform. The attractiveness of Israel as a business partner has become so powerful that it is being deployed as a geopolitical tool under the name of "innovation diplomacy" to help the Jewish state build ties with historical enemies.[61]

America's competitors have also realized that our investment in Israel has given us a valuable economic partner. Russia, for example, has worked to maintain a close relationship with Israel based on the Soviet role in liberating Europe from the Nazis and on its sales of weapons to the Jewish state immediately after it was established. But the most powerful connection between Israel and Russia is demographic, as some 15 percent of Israelis are of Russian descent.

Of course, the reason there are so many Russian Jews in Israel is not a happy one. Soviet Russia was an authoritarian atheist state that suppressed religious identity and aggressively persecuted Jews. Russian Jews started to immigrate to Israel after 1972, although so many were denied permission to leave that they were dubbed the "refusniks." Eventually American human-rights champions such as Senator Henry "Scoop" Jackson, a Democrat from Washington, and President Ronald Reagan applied pressure on the Soviets, and more emigration was permitted until the restrictions were lifted altogether and large numbers flooded into Israel.[62] Nevertheless, Moscow still tries to take advantage of its demographic ties with Israel to complicate America's relationship with a key ally. President Vladimir Putin visited the Jewish state in 2020 for the dedication of a memorial to the siege of Leningrad,[63] for example, and

Israel has played a somewhat equivocal role on the issue of the Russian invasion of Ukraine.

But an even more powerful U.S. competitor has turned its eyes to Israel over the past twenty years: China. Although there has been little engagement between the two countries historically, China now sees Israel as a potential component of its global infrastructure development strategy known as the Belt and Road Initiative, which Israel too originally viewed as an opportunity.[64] Beijing has also tried to exploit Israel as a backdoor source of sensitive technology that has become increasingly guarded by the United States. China has provided Israel with a small but growing source of foreign direct investment (FDI), on which Israel's start-up culture depends, and has been a competitive bidder on key infrastructure projects that European and American companies passed over for security reasons.

After hovering between five hundred million and two billion dollars per year for a decade, Chinese FDI ballooned to almost six billion dollars per year in 2016.[65] This increase got the attention of the incoming Trump administration, which was concerned that if it were permitted to grow unchecked and largely without oversight, it could constitute an intolerable penetration of the U.S.–Israel security and intelligence partnership. Israel recognized this danger as well, and Chinese FDI went down to $260 million a year or less under President Trump but went back up to two billion dollars in the first year of the Biden administration. China has also dangerously insinuated itself into critical Israeli infrastructure by winning the contract to manage Haifa port on the Mediterranean, where U.S. Navy vessels have routinely docked.[66]

As China has cemented a more formal partnership with Russia and Iran, however, clear incompatibilities with Israel have emerged that may well end substantial cooperation. For while Israel has long, if somewhat uneasy, ties with Russia, Iran has been an implacable foe dedicated to the eradication of the Jewish state since 1979. As economically advantageous as cooperation with China might have seemed in the past, the Chinese companies that have won major contracts for Israeli projects are also working in Iran, presenting Israel with a security dilemma that has made it increasingly skeptical of working with China.[67]

The United States should welcome the souring of ties between Israel and China as an opportunity to protect a critical economic and technological partner from infiltration by a hostile competitor. The China–Russia–Iran axis, opposed to the United States and its allies in Europe and Asia, presents Israel with a decision between these two camps that will have to be made in the not-too-distant future—if it has not already been made—especially if America energetically expands economic cooperation with Israel as a matter of national security.[68]

CHAPTER THREE:
SEARCHING FOR AN ALTERNATIVE:
A HERITAGE OF FAILURE

The Perils of Equivocation

THERE APPEARS TO be an almost irresistible American compulsion to try to resolve the Israel–Palestinian issue at the end of a presidential term. In the case of Ronald Reagan, it came in December 1988 when Secretary of State George Shultz recognized the Palestine Liberation Organization (PLO) as a legitimate negotiating partner for a peace deal with Israel.[1]

Shultz had prioritized progress on Middle East peace during Reagan's second term, traveling to the region repeatedly and trying to leverage his relationship with Prime Minister Yitzhak Shamir to get the Israelis to make more concessions to the PLO. Shamir, who had been born in Poland and lost his parents and two sisters in the Holocaust, was a follower of Jabotinsky. He fought alongside the paramilitary Zionist groups and worked for the Israeli intelligence service Mossad after the foundation of the Jewish state. After joining the Likud party, he was elected to the Knesset in 1973, eventually becoming Begin's foreign minister and successor as chairman of the party. He served as prime minister from 1983 to 1984 and from 1986 to 1992.

While Shamir was prime minister, the Palestinians launched a new type of attack on Israel. After the humiliating defeat in the Yom Kippur War and the subsequent peace accord between Egypt and Israel, another coordinated Arab attack on Israel seemed unlikely. While relations between the Jewish state and neighbors such as Syria and Lebanon remained fractious and would periodically flare into war, the other relationships were increasingly calm. There was therefore little real pressure on Israel to return any of the territory it had seized in the Six-Day War some twenty years before in the West Bank, Gaza, and the Golan Heights.

The Palestinians tried to take things into their own hands. The PLO, which had been led by Yasser Arafat since 1969, had launched sporadic terrorist attacks on Israel first from Jordan and then from Lebanon. The Arab world largely accepted the PLO as the *de facto* leadership of the Palestinians, but relations were always contentious. (The PLO was expelled from Jordan in 1971.) The PLO itself was internally conflicted. Arafat's faction, Fatah, was the largest, but the organization also included the Popular Front for the Liberation of Palestine (PFLP) and the Democratic Front for the Liberation of Palestine (DFLP), among others. These divisions made it difficult for the Palestinians to reach a consensus and for the rest of the world to understand who was speaking for whom.

Arafat did take actions that might have indicated he was seriously interested in a peace deal, such as recognizing two U.N. Security Council resolutions: 242, which had called for the end of the Six-Day War in 1967, and 338, which had called for the end of the Yom Kippur War in 1973. This move suggested the PLO had abandoned its stated mission to eradicate Israel and would accept a two-state solution. But these green shoots were meager, and at the same time, Arafat continued to pursue political ends with direct terrorist violence against Israeli civilians. In 1987, the PLO coordinated a popular rebellion and launched the First Intifada, or "uprising," a series of internal attacks on Israel from Palestinian positions in the West Bank and Gaza. Not a conventional military action, the Intifada consisted of sporadic violence, including throwing stones and Molotov cocktails in a general effort to terrorize Israel into concessions.

The Intifada was a grave mistake for the Palestinians. After the Yom Kippur War, and particularly after the 1979 peace deal with Egypt, economic activity between Israel and the Palestinians had grown. Some 40 percent of the Palestinian workforce had jobs in Israel before 1987. There was still much work to be done to increase Palestinian access to higher-level employment, but the potential was there to get to political normalization through economic cooperation. The Intifada destroyed any such path forward, as it included strikes, boycotts of Israeli goods, and the refusal to pay taxes that deliberately undermined the nascent progress.

Seeing Prime Minister Shamir's increasing resistance to any concessions to the Palestinians as the Intifada ground on, and hoping to break the stalemate, Secretary of State Shultz decided to recognize the legitimacy of the PLO. But as was so often the case in the peace process, the action was equivocal. One *Washington Post* headline said the United States had "in effect" recognized the PLO. The State Department said this was merely an indication of America's engaging in a "substantive dialogue" with the Palestinians. The United States had continued to reject Arafat's unilateral declaration of a Palestinian state earlier in 1988, and just weeks before the de facto recognition of the PLO, Shultz himself denied Arafat a visa to visit the United Nations in New York on the grounds that he was a terrorist.[2] Shultz's diplomatic "Hail Mary" pass did not result in peace and only succeeded in further muddying the murky waters of the Middle East. It was harbinger of what was to come in the next two U.S. administrations.

The Slow-Motion Diplomatic Fiasco

EMBARKING IN THE 1990s on a period of rapid economic growth and increasing global prominence, Israel was eager to get the Palestinian issue resolved. The United States wanted a deal. The Europeans wanted a deal. The United Nations wanted a deal. But the fundamental problem was that in 1990, Secretary Shultz's action notwithstanding, there was no legitimate Palestinian leadership with which a deal could be made, and the next two decades of trying to wish one into existence were a slow-motion diplomatic fiasco. The PLO was never really a viable option. It had none of the components of classical statehood. At best it was a cause, but its only organizing principal was the eradication of another successful state that had to date decisively defeated all the Palestinians' attempts to destroy it. The PLO was never held accountable for this failure, however, and no one in a position of authority informed it that any negotiations with Israel were not between two equal parties but in fact between the victor and the defeated.

The unwillingness to recognize this reality doomed from the outset the agreements that would become known as the Oslo Accords. The intentions behind them were of course good. The George H. W. Bush administration, preoccupied with the fall of the Berlin Wall and the collapse of the Soviet Union and then by the Iraqi invasion of Kuwait, did not at first prioritize the Palestinian issue. Arafat spectacularly mismanaged Iraq by supporting Saddam Hussein even though the rest of the Arab League condemned the invasion and more than 350,000 Palestinians living in Kuwait were displaced by Saddam's aggression.[3] Furthermore, the most vehement Arab opponents of Iraq's invasion included not only Kuwait itself but also the other wealthy Gulf states that were then some of the PLO's main sources of support.

Even before the U.S.-led coalition's military intervention to push the Iraqis out of Kuwait, Saddam attacked Israel with Scud missiles on the grounds that Israel was an American proxy. U.S-made Patriot missile-defense systems intercepted some of the Scuds, but a number got through, and two Israelis were killed. To preserve the international coalition, which included Arab partners, however, the United States pressured Israel to not retaliate. Then, in an address to Congress at the conclusion of the first Gulf War in March 1991, President Bush laid out his vision for the Middle East, announcing,

> A comprehensive peace must be grounded in United Nations Security Council Resolutions 242 and 338 and the principle of territory for peace. This principle must be elaborated to provide for Israel's security and recognition, and at the same time for legitimate Palestinian political rights. Anything else would fail the twin tests of fairness and security. The time has come to put an end to Arab–Israeli conflict.[4]

The president made no mention of the PLO's support for Saddam in the war the United States had just won. Instead, he put the world on notice that Israel would have to cede territory to the Palestinians if it hoped for peace. Then, in retaliation for what the United States interpreted as aggressive Israeli settlement activity in the West Bank, Bush withheld some eleven billion dollars in loan guarantees to Israel to assist with the assimilation of Russian émigrés into the Jewish state. The guarantees were reinstated only when Israel agreed to participate in the Madrid Conference of 1991, co-sponsored by the United States and a moribund Soviet Union, which was to dissolve in a matter of months.

The practical results of Madrid were predictably thin, but the conference did bring about a bilateral dialogue between Israel and Jordan, which should have been a signal that bilateral deals between nation-states might be the more practical path to peace going forward. While the ambitious multilateral agenda of Madrid morphed into the bloated Oslo process, there were excellent reasons to pursue a smaller but concrete Israel–Jordan deal. The new American president, Bill Clinton, although inexperienced in foreign affairs and confronting a new geopolitical reality after the Cold War, recognized the political benefits of sealing the second Israel–Arab normalization treaty.

Like President Carter before him, President Clinton was dealing with an unorthodox pair of peace partners. On the Jordanian side he had King Hussein, who had inherited his father's throne in 1953 and spent the next twenty years at war with Israel—in fact, he was almost assassinated by Israel during the Six-Day War. A Hashemite claiming direct descent from Muhammad, Hussein had a personal interest in Jerusalem, the site of the Prophet's ascent to heaven and thus the third-holiest site for Islam.

On the Israeli side, Clinton was dealing with the new prime minister, Yitzhak Rabin, the first premier to be born in Israel. He had served with distinction in the IDF and had been among the first soldiers into the Old City of Jerusalem in 1967. He had been ambassador to the United States before becoming prime minister in 1992, the same year Clinton was elected president. Later that year, he received an honorary doctorate from Hebrew University and in his acceptance speech reflected on the war:

It all starts and ends with the spirit. Our soldiers prevailed not by their weapons but by their awareness of their supreme mission, by their awareness of the righteousness of their cause, by their deep love for their homeland and by their recognition of the difficult task laid upon them—to ensure the existence of our people in our homeland, to defend, even at the price of their own lives, the right of the Jewish people to live in their own state, free, independent and in peace.[5]

Prospects for a treaty between Hussein and Rabin may well have seemed slim at the beginning. A relatively a young state, founded in 1923, Jordan had been the recipient of significant numbers of Palestinian refugees after 1948 and took in another wave after 1967. But after Jordan expelled the PLO in the early 1970s, the country's increasing reliance on security and economic assistance from the United States gave Clinton leverage.

Rabin was also a different Israeli politician from his more conservative predecessor, Yitzhak Shamir. A member of the Labor party, he had succeeded Golda Meir as prime minister in 1974 (serving until 1977) and became premier again in 1992. Rabin had already demonstrated considerably more flexibility regarding concessions for peace, and in the Oslo Accords, which had been signed in 1993, had officially recognized the PLO. Perhaps from their experience of fighting against each other, Hussein and Rabin seemed to understand that the futures of Israel and Jordan were intertwined and that they might now need to depend on each other for survival.[6]

Over time Hussein and Rabin formed a friendship based on trust. President Clinton had originally hoped to include Syria's President Hafez al-Assad in a broader peace deal, but when Assad proved less amenable to the necessary concessions and more demanding of Washington, negotiations were limited to Israel and Jordan. At the White House on July 25, 1994, Hussein and Rabin signed the Washington Declaration, affirming their commitment to formalize relations and negotiate a treaty that would end the state of war between the two countries that had existed since 1948.

The actual agreement, signed three months later on the Israel–Jordan border by the prime ministers of both countries and witnessed by President Clinton himself, was considerably broader than the previous agreement between Israel and Egypt. This deal included not only the cessation of hostilities but also agreements on issues such as water rights and supply, as well as drug trafficking and refugees. In addition, the treaty established the "special role" of the Hashemite monarch in the Muslim shrines in Jerusalem.[7]

Though not an unmitigated success, the Israel–Jordan deal has been undeniably beneficial to both countries, particularly because of the security cooperation that has grown with U.S. support, and it has endured. Much more can and should be done in the future—increasing Jordan's access to Israeli-generated desalinated water and electricity, for example— but the agreement remains a signature diplomatic achievement for the Clinton administration.[8]

The same cannot be said, unfortunately, of President Clinton's other major Middle East initiative, the Oslo Accords. This process emerged from George H. W. Bush's Madrid conference with the goal of establishing a comprehensive framework for the coexistence of Israel and a Palestinian entity. The negotiations in Oslo were formally announced at the White House in October 1993, the first year of Clinton's presidency, and the elusive pursuit of a final agreement would occupy him through the last days of his second term.

For his part, Prime Minister Rabin was prepared to make considerable concessions to get to a Palestinian deal, beginning with freezing Jewish settlements in the West Bank, and at first Oslo appeared destined for success. But the process was hampered by a fundamental flaw: Israel and the PLO were not equal negotiating partners as nation-states. Chairman Yasser Arafat was simply did not have the authority of a President Sadat or King Hussein to make a deal, even if he had wanted to.

Arafat was born to a Palestinian family in Egypt some time in 1929, but that is almost the only fact known for certain about his early life. He later crafted his autobiography to suit his self-proclaimed role as the champion of the Palestinian people, claiming to have fought in the 1948 war after the establishment of Israel. In 1959 he participated in the founding of Fatah, a political and paramilitary organization dedicated to organizing Palestinian, as opposed to pan-Arab, opposition to Israel, and coordinated terrorist attacks on Israel expanded shortly thereafter. Black September, an elite strike force within Fatah, was formed in 1970 primarily to destabilize Jordan. Designed to give Fatah plausible deniability for its crimes, Black September was nevertheless widely understood to be an "extension" of Fatah.[9]

Black September went into international action at the 1972 Munich Olympics. Eight terrorists infiltrated the Olympic Village, where they grotesquely executed two members of the Israeli delegation and took an additional nine hostages. The Germans' attempted rescue failed, and all the hostages were killed. Captured on live television for maximum shock value, the attack was launched with the tacit permission if not the direct approval, of the head of Fatah, Yasser Arafat.[10]

Just two years later, clad in his signature black and white keffiyeh (*The New York Times* gushed about his "desert garb"[11]), Arafat became the first representative of a nongovernmental organization to address the United Nations General Assembly. The 1974 invitation implied that Arafat represented the equivalent of a nation-state, and while he did not sit in the beige armchair reserved for heads of state, he stood behind it with his arm on the back for the speech.[12] Arafat took the opportunity to make a direct appeal for support to the American people and associate the Palestinian cause with U.S. independence:

> I cannot now forgo this opportunity to appeal from this rostrum directly to the American people, asking it to give its support to our heroic and fighting people. I ask it wholeheartedly to endorse right and justice, to recall George Washington to mind, heroic Washington whose purpose was his nation's freedom and independence, Abraham Lincoln, champion of the destitute and the wretched, and also Woodrow Wilson, whose doctrine

of Fourteen Points remains subscribed to and venerated by our people. I ask the American people whether the demonstrations of hostility and enmity taking place outside this great hall reflect the true intent of America's will. What crime, I ask you plainly, has our people committed against the American people? Why do you fight us so? Does such unwarranted belligerence really serve your interests? Does it serve the interests of the American masses? No, definitely not. I can only hope that the American people will remember that their friendship with the whole Arab nation is too great, too abiding and too rewarding for any such demonstrations to harm it.[13]

Fifty years ago, Arafat thus laid the foundation for the pro-Hamas response to October 7, 2023, in America, appropriating the American founders, notably Washington, for the Palestinian cause and making Israel, and Jews in general, who opposed the invitation for a terrorist mastermind to speak at the United Nations, the agents of "enmity and hostility." In spite of Arafat's vows to eradicate Israel, his culpability in any number of terrorist attacks on Israelis, and his virulently antisemitic views and endemic personal corruption, his message resonated with the Marxist Left in the United States, which hailed him as a hero. Arafat departed New York shortly thereafter for Cuba. His visit to the United Nations set the trajectory of that body firmly on the pro-Palestinian, anti-Israel tack on which it remains today. The following year the United Nations General Assembly passed Resolution 3379, which defined Zionism as a form of racial discrimination, which was seen as a significant victory for the PLO and their Soviet and Arab backers.[14]

The resolution was in fact the product of the antisemitism of all these groups, which were looking for a way to defend their own bigotry by blaming the Jews for it. It was so internally conflicted and irrational that it was repealed sixteen years later after the end of the Cold War, but not before *Saturday Night Live*, not a noted bastion of conservatism, lampooned it on "Weekend Update with Chevy Chase":

The United Nations General Assembly passed a resolution equating Zionism with racism. Black entertainer Sammy Davis, Jr., a convert to Judaism, was quoted as saying: "What a breakthrough! Now, finally, I can hate myself!"[15]

Terrorist attacks by Black September and related groups continued under Arafat's leadership and grabbed international headlines. In 1985, for example, on orders from Arafat's office in Tunisia, members of the Palestinian Liberation Front (PLF) hijacked the *Achille Lauro,* an Italian cruise ship in the Mediterranean off the coast of Egypt.[16] They shot the wheelchair-bound elderly American Leon Klinghoffer and dumped his body overboard because he was Jewish. The *Achille Lauro* was eventually liberated and some of the hijackers were tried in Italian courts, but the main architects of the atrocity, Arafat and Mohammad Zaidan, the head of the PLF, escaped justice. The terrorist attacks continued.

In the absence of any other Palestinian leadership, Arafat established himself as the face of the PLO, a status that Secretary Shultz confirmed, despite his personal antipathy. When President Clinton resumed the peace process in 1992, Arafat was therefore the default choice of negotiating partner for Israel in Oslo. And while he did seem to recognize the right of Israel to exist and paid lip service to renouncing the goal of eradicating Israel and replacing it with a Palestinian state, this position was always somewhat qualified.[17] Arafat also did not seem to speak with the full backing of all the Palestinian factions.

After a first round of secret negotiations, Rabin, Arafat, and Clinton met on the south lawn of the White House in September 1993 for a historic photo-op, smiling and clasping hands as they signed "Oslo I." Arafat, Rabin, and the Israeli foreign minister, Shimon Peres, shared a Nobel Peace Prize in 1994, and crowds of negotiators descended on Oslo for months of talks resulting in "Oslo II." A concrete deal such as the one between Israel and Jordan, however, proved elusive. The framework was simply unrealistic. Having defeated the Arabs decisively in 1973, Israel denied the PLO its safe havens in Jordan and Lebanon, only to see the First Intifada launched in the 1980s. But according to the provisions of Oslo, Israel was now preparing to recognize some degree of Palestinian self-governance in the West Bank and Gaza. It even agreed to the establishment of an armed Palestinian security force, though the Palestinians had no system of government and factions such as Hamas and PLF opposed any compromise that left Israel intact.

Israelis were deeply divided about the deal being negotiated in Oslo, many of them seeing Prime Minister Rabin as a traitor to the Zionist cause. Demonstrations by both sides were increasingly incendiary, and in October 1995 Rabin was assassinated by an Israeli nationalist after a pro-Oslo rally in Tel Aviv. Ongoing political turmoil over the issue in Israel then resulted in a rapid succession of prime ministers, from Shimon Peres of the Labor Party, appointed to succeed Rabin, to Benjamin Netanyahu of Likud, elected in 1996, to Ehud Barak of Labor in 1999.

President Clinton, nearing the end of his scandal-ridden second term and in search of a legacy, hoped he had found in Barak an Israeli leader like Begin, one who was willing to make significant concessions to get to a peace deal. In the summer of 2000, he invited Barak and Arafat to Camp David in an attempt to recapture the success Carter had achieved there with Begin and Sadat twenty years earlier, but to no avail. Barak had come ready to negotiate, but Arafat was intractable. Then, shortly before Christmas, after the disputed presidential election had been resolved, Clinton brought the Israeli and Palestinian negotiating teams to the White House and read them the outlines of a deal that became known as the "Clinton Parameters":

On territory, I recommended 94 to 96 percent of the West Bank for the Palestinians with a land swap from Israel of 1 to 3 percent, and an understanding that the land kept by Israel would include 80 percent of the settlers in blocs. On security, I said Israeli forces should withdraw over a three-year period while an international force would be gradually introduced, with the understanding that a small Israeli presence in the Jordan Valley could remain for another three years under the authority of the international forces. The Israelis would also be able to maintain their early-warning station in the West Bank with a Palestinian liaison presence. In the event of an "imminent and demonstrable threat to Israel's security," there would be provision for emergency deployments in the West Bank.

The new state of Palestine would be "nonmilitarized," but would have a strong security force; sovereignty over its airspace, with special arrangement to meet Israeli training and operational needs; and an international force for border security and deterrence.

On Jerusalem, I recommended that the Arab neighborhoods be in Palestine and the Jewish neighborhoods in Israel, and that the Palestinians should have sovereignty over the Temple Mount/ Haram and the Israelis sovereignty over the Western Wall and the "holy space" of which it is a part with no excavation around the wall or under the Mount at least without mutual consent.

On refugees, I said that the new state of Palestine should be the homeland for refugees displaced in the 1948 war and afterward, without ruling out the possibility that Israel would accept some of the refugees according to its own laws and sovereign decisions, giving priority to the refugee populations in Lebanon. I recommended an international effort to compensate refugees and assist them in finding houses in the new state of Palestine, in the land-swap areas to be transferred to Palestine, in their current host countries, in other willing nations, or in Israel. Both parties should agree that this solution would satisfy United Nations Resolution 194.

Finally, the agreement had to clearly mark the end of the conflict and put an end to all violence. I suggested a new U.N. resolution saying that this agreement, along with the final release of Palestinian prisoners, would fulfill the requirements of resolutions 242 and 338.[18]

These terms should have been extraordinarily attractive to the Palestinians. They would have given them a state, including parts of Jerusalem, largely on the lines of the 1967 borders and with some provision for the refugees, which is what they had said they wanted. Barak accepted it. But in the end, Arafat, as he had done at Camp David, said no.

Clinton noted in his autobiography that he had found Arafat increasingly diminished during their engagements in 2000, speculating that he was losing his mental capacity to explain why he didn't take the deal, even when it was supported by the Jordanians, Egyptians, and Saudis.[19] A harder but perhaps more accurate rationale is that Arafat refused the offer because he knew it wasn't what the Palestinian people would accept. After years of being told they were the equivalent of the Israelis and bolstered by billions of dollars of foreign aid, they were still in what Jabotinsky might have called a "Plan-A mindset" according to which their goal was the eradication of the Jewish state, not the establishment of their own alongside it. The American president had offered them essentially what their public position had been, but that turned out not to be what the Palestinians really wanted. Clinton's final effort failed, and the Second Intifada of terrorist attacks on Israel, which had begun after the Camp David meetings, intensified.

In a harbinger of what was to come eight years later, a member of Clinton's National Security Council staff, Robert Malley, and one of the Palestinian negotiators, Hussein Agha, wrote a long-form piece challenging the conventional wisdom (held by Clinton himself, as well as his lead negotiator, Dennis Ross) that the Camp David deal had been essentially everything the Palestinians had said they wanted and that Barak had been willing to compromise, while Arafat was obstinate. According to Malley and Agha, Arafat had been offended by Barak's early prioritization of a deal with Syria rather than with the Palestinians and had other good reasons to distrust the prime minister, who he believed was in a conspiracy with Clinton against the Palestinians.

As Malley and Agha's account unfolds, Ehud Barak emerges as a master manipulator who seems to promise everything while in fact offering nothing, while Arafat is bullied by the more powerful into engaging in a process he is only trying to survive. For its part, the United States was hamstrung by internal conflicts resulting from its cultural affinity and strategic relationship with Israel, which legitimized the Palestinians' deep suspicion of America. In the end, Malley and Agha conclude that all three parties had their legitimate perspectives, and that no one was really to blame for the failure. In the Obama administration, Malley, who had gone to high school with Vice President Biden's national security advisor, Antony Blinken, and law school with Obama himself, would play an important role in shaping the new president's policy, and in 2021 he became President Biden's special envoy for Iran.

One lasting legacy of Clinton's Oslo initiative was the establishment of the Palestinian Authority, which would become the official governing mechanism for the territories. Originally intended to govern for a five-year period, 1995–2000, the PA remains in control of the West Bank some quarter of a century later, having held no elections since 2006. Arafat died in 2004, and his place was taken by Mahmoud Abbas, now in the eighteenth year of his original four-year term. Abbas, corrupt and unpopular, survives because, once again, in the absence of an alternative, the international community insists on treating him as a head of state and the legitimate partner for any negotiations with Israel.

The Uniparty Strikes Again

THE GEORGE W. BUSH administration ended in an ignominious scramble at the United Nations Security Council. Having begun with an election whose legitimacy had been hotly disputed, the administration was ending in disappointment. A historic financial crisis and the apparently endless conflicts in Afghanistan and Iraq after 9/11 had given the Democrats the victory in the presidential election of 2008. Democrat Barack Obama would succeed President Bush in the White House in what could only be seen as an electoral repudiation of his second term. The Bush administration was desperate for a success on its way out the door.

Secretary of State Condoleezza Rice concluded that a breakthrough in the Israel–Palestinian peace process—particularly after Iraq soured in 2005—might burnish the administration's legacy.[20] Secretary Rice had tried with the Annapolis meetings in November 2008 to achieve the peace deal President Clinton had failed to achieve at Camp David eight years earlier.[21] But the new Palestinian leadership proved no more cooperative than the old, and although the new Israeli prime minister, Ehud Olmert, offered significant concessions, Abbas would not come to terms.

Despite Israel's voluntary withdrawal (with U.S. encouragement) from Gaza in 2005, the south of the country remained volatile. Hamas, elected the next year to run Gaza, continued to stockpile weapons and fighters in the strip. At the end of 2008, fighting flared, resulting in Israel's Operation Cast Lead, designed to neutralize the rockets Hamas was firing on civilian Israeli targets. Then as now, Hamas used the civilians in Gaza as human shields, and the inevitable casualties provoked international outrage and condemnation of Israel.

In January 2009, Secretary Rice and the U.N. Security Council proposed Resolution 1860, calling for an immediate ceasefire on which she planned to vote in the affirmative.[22] At the last minute, on the recommendation of National Security Advisor Steve Hadley and his deputy, Elliott Abrams, President Bush ordered her to stand down.[23] But Bush did not insist that Rice vote against the resolution, which, given America's veto, would have scuttled it. The resolution was adopted, and the United States' abstention on the vote by a Republican administration, its first since the 1960s, sent Hamas the message that there was bipartisan support for their cause in America.

Pivot to Iran: The Obama Legacy

BUSH'S SUCCESSOR, BARACK OBAMA, took a radically new approach to the Middle East in general and to the Palestinian issue in particular in his pursuit of an alternative to Israel as a strategic partner for the United States, looking not only to the Palestinians but also to the Islamic Republic of Iran.

Partnership between Iran and the United States was not unprecedented, as under Shah Mohammad Reza Pahlavi, who reigned from 1941 to 1979, there was strong cooperation between the two countries—as well as between Iran and Israel. All of that changed in 1979 with the revolution that deposed the shah and installed a Shiite theocracy in his place. Most Americans' first encounter with the new regime came when the revolutionaries took fifty-two diplomats at the U.S. embassy in Tehran hostage and held them for 444 days.

President Jimmy Carter may have had a preview of what was brewing in Iran, as recently declassified records suggest he might have been in communication with the radical Ayatollah Ruhollah Khomeini, who was living in Paris but determined to return to Iran and replace the shah.[24] Khomeini reportedly assured Carter before the revolution that he commanded the support of the Iranian people and would continue to be a friend to America if the president persuaded the shah to leave the country. This proposal would have appealed to Carter, who had prioritized human rights over American national-security interests in his foreign policy. As events unfolded, however, Carter was shocked by the establishment of a radical-Islamist regime dedicated to the eradication of Israel and the United States.

It was no coincidence that the American hostages in Tehran were released on January 20, 1981, the day Ronald Reagan replaced Carter as president. Though the new administration took a dim view of Tehran, it eventually made the mistake of engaging with the regime in what became known as the "Iran–Contra affair." This attempt to strike a backdoor deal with Iran to offset the greater evil—totalitarian communism—should have served as a warning that no good would come of engaging with the mullahs even with the best of intentions.

George H.W. Bush and Bill Clinton largely steered clear of Iran during their presidencies, although Clinton did initiate a presidential commission to study Iran's developing missile program. In the 1990s, the regime's increasing offensive capabilities, rumored to be connected to the clandestine pursuit of nuclear weapons, were already a concern.

The bipartisan Commission to Assess the Ballistic Missile Threat to the United States, chaired by Donald Rumsfeld, reached the consensus that the threat to America from these weapons, particularly in the hands of Iran, was much more acute than was indicated by recent intelligence reports, and the United States needed to aggressively develop missile defense capabilities to counter them.[25]

This concern about the threat from Tehran was still strong on both sides of the aisle in the Congress when Barack Obama assumed office in January 2009, but the new president took a different view. Having concluded that the now-traditional robust U.S. support for Israel had failed to bring peace, his administration sought to influence affairs in the Middle East by engaging with Iran. The rationale was that if the United States curbed its aggressive behavior, which had a terrible track record in Iraq and Afghanistan and listened to other powers, the region would naturally become more stable.

Obama was from his student days connected with the radicals who had developed Critical Race Theory in the 1960s, notably Bill and Bernadine Ayers, founders of the Weather Underground movement and, many years later, prominent visitors to the pro-Hamas encampment at the University of Chicago after the October 7, 2023, attacks.[26] Perhaps more influential was the attorney and civil rights activist Derrick Bell, one of Obama's professors at Harvard Law School. Bell's writings explore what he identified as the endemic racism of the United States in a series of Socratic dialogues with a fictional interlocutor named Geneva Crenshaw:

In "The Chronicle of the Constitutional Contradiction," for example, "Crenshaw" questioned framers of the Constitution and the compromises they made for slavery, in particular the counting of three-fifths of the enumerated population of slaves to enhance the white Southern representation in Congress. By highlighting that moral compromise, "Crenshaw" correctly identified the constitutional snake in the garden of "originalism" (the commitment among conservative judges to interpreting

the modern Constitution based exclusively on what the founders thought).[27]

At a 1990 rally in support of Bell, Obama urged the audience "to open
their hearts and minds" to his work.[28]

During the Obama administration, the Central Intelligence Agency
publicly asserted that it had played an important role in the 1953 coup
that removed the Iranian prime minister Mohammad Mossadegh
and consolidated power in the hands of the shah.[29] In the podcast *The
Langley Files*, CIA agents referred to the coup as one of the few instances when the agency had undermined a democratically elected leader.
While responsible historians dispute this assertion, pointing to evidence
that the coup was internally driven,[30] the narrative that America had
destroyed Iran's democracy and has only its imperialist self to blame for
the subsequent enmity between the two countries took hold.[31] Obama
appeared to be trying to atone for this historical sin through conciliatory outreach to the Iranian regime while downgrading the United States'
relationship with its fellow oppressor Israel.

The president made his approach explicit in a speech he gave at Cairo
University in the opening months of his administration. Titled "A New
Beginning," the address was designed to reset the U.S. approach to
the Islamic world as the attacks of 9/11 became more distant in time.
Military intervention and political meddling would be things of the
past, while respectful cooperation would be the new normal.[32] Though
he acknowledged the Holocaust, Obama made no mention of the value
of the modern U.S.–Israel alliance. He declared, "if we see this conflict
only from one side or the other, then we will be blind to the truth: The
only resolution is for the aspirations of both sides to be met through two
states, where Israelis and Palestinians each live in peace and security."

Turning to Iran, the president acknowledged U.S. culpability in the
1953 coup, then proposed a new path. "Rather than remain trapped in
the past," Obama said,

I've made it clear to Iran's leaders and people that my country is prepared to move forward. The question now is not what Iran is against, but rather what future it wants to build. I recognize it will be hard to overcome decades of mistrust, but we will proceed with courage, rectitude, and resolve. There will be many issues to discuss between our two countries, and we are willing to move forward without preconditions on the basis of mutual respect.

Obama's signature soaring rhetoric provoked a rapturous response from the crowd ("We love you Barack Obama!"). But what he did *not* say in Cairo was as telling as what he did say—there was no mention of the Iranian people or their aspirations for liberty. Yet a week later, Iran erupted in what became known as the Green Revolution, the most intense anti-regime protests in twenty years.

The uneasy reality since 1979 in Iran was that the regime, though powerful, was not as popular as Khomeini had predicted before the revolution. The Iranian people had been used to a secular, Westernized way of life under the shah and were proud of their Persian heritage and culture. Demonstrations against the authoritarian theocratic mullahs were not infrequent, and in June 2009 they broke out in earnest.

Nominally a republic, Iran is in fact tightly controlled by a small group of radical Shiite clerics known as the Guardian Council, headed by Supreme Leader Ali Khamenei, who succeeded Khomeini in 1989. By controlling who can run for office, the council controls the outcome of any "election," and should there nevertheless be an unfortunate result, the ministry of the interior can adjust the vote count as necessary. On June 12, 2009, it was announced that the council's chosen candidate, Mahmoud Ahmadinejad, had won reelection to the presidency by a two-to-one margin against his closest competitor, Mir-Hossein Mousavi. While hardly a champion of democracy, Mousavi had some claim to being more reformist than the hardline Ahmadinejad, and there was a pervasive conviction among the Iranian people that the election was intolerably and obviously rigged. They poured into the streets by the millions, demanding "Where is my vote?" after Mousavi declared that millions of ballots were missing.[33] The "Green Movement," named for the color of Mousavi's sash, was born.

Thanks to their smartphones, the protestors could coordinate and communicate, both with each other and the outside world. Pictures of the crowds surging through the streets of Tehran and across the entire country made headlines. Some of the signs were in English, calling out for America and Obama to help them.[34]

Given Obama's campaign theme of "hope and change," it might have seemed an easy call for the administration to energetically support the protests. The Iranian regime, which had been a growing problem for the United States, was widely believed to be clandestinely developing a nuclear weapon. The standard chant on official occasions was "Death to America" followed by "Death to Israel," and the regime referred to these two adversaries as the Great Satan and the Little Satan, respectively. This nihilistic rhetoric made the mullahs' pursuit of a nuke all the more dangerous.

Having caught the regime off guard, the Green Movement seemed at first to have the upper hand. Quickly enough, however, the crackdown began. The Islamic Revolutionary Guard Corps (IRGC) and the Basij paramilitary brigades sprang into action. Protestors were beaten, detained, and then shot by snipers. One young woman, Neda Soltan, was filmed as she bled to death on a sidewalk after being targeted.[35] As it had been thirty years earlier, Iran seemed on the brink of revolution.

Yet Obama remained resolutely silent for days. When he did finally speak, it was in platitudes. He assured the people of Iran that "[t]hose who stand up for justice are always on the right side of history," and he called Soltan's death "heartbreaking." But as for doing anything to help, he bowed out, offering the excuse that if he acted, the regime would blame the United States and the uprising would fail.[36]

Obama's reticence produced that same result, however. The regime immediately and predictably blamed the United States for stirring up the protests as it had blamed America for all its woes since 1979, and without U.S. support, the protests did fail. As it turned out, for the president, unrest in Iran was deeply inconvenient because, as was evidenced in the Cairo speech, he had already established a policy of engaging with Tehran as an equal negotiating partner and without preconditions. For this scenario to work, the regime had to be seen as stable and legitimate, a status the Green Revolution dangerously threatened.

Many Americans, especially those old enough to remember the 1979 hostage crisis, were puzzled. After disappointments in Afghanistan and Iraq, where promised peaceful democracies had failed to materialize after the U.S. invasion, the American people were rightly skeptical of externally imposed regime change in the Middle East. But if the Iranian people were trying on their own to topple a government that was hostile to the United States and Israel and in command of an increasingly capable military, it seemed obvious that vocal support, at least, was called for.

Senator John Kerry of Massachusetts, the Democrat chairman of the Senate Foreign Relations Committee, took to the editorial page of *The New York Times* to explain Obama's grand strategy. In "With Iran, Think Before You Speak," Kerry darkly referred to the "1953 American-sponsored coup" and argued that any U.S. involvement would render Mousavi "a Western puppet." Obama, on the other hand,

> ... has made that clear in devising a new approach to Iran and the wider Muslim world. In offering negotiation and conciliation, he has put the region's extremists on the defensive. We have seen the results of this new vision already. His outreach may have helped to make a difference in the election last week in Lebanon, where a pro-Western coalition surprised many by winning a resounding victory. We're seeing signs that it's having an impact in Iran as well. Returning to harsh criticism now would only erase this progress, empower hard-liners in Iran who want to see negotiations fail and undercut those who have risen up in support of a better relationship.[37]

Kerry's opinion piece sent the chilling message that any reform in Iran would have to come from within the regime, not from the Iranian people.

In Israel, Benjamin Netanyahu, who had won a new term as prime minister shortly after Obama's inauguration in 2009, was increasingly focused on Iran's nuclear ambitions, which he saw as the primary regional threat to the Jewish state. In their first meeting at the White House in May 2009, Obama assured Netanyahu that his Iran policy would be "dual-track," combining direct engagement with the threat of sanctions if the regime refused to negotiate. The president proposed giving this approach a year before pivoting to sanctions, promising that a military strike was being prepared to take care of the nuclear program should the negotiations fail.[38] In addition, Obama frankly informed Jewish leaders that he would no longer adhere to George W. Bush's policy of "no daylight" between Israel and the United States. Eight years of that policy had not resulted in peace, and a more open airing of differences, he thought, might make progress.[39]

The Israelis remained concerned about the president's engagement with Iran, and in March 2010 Obama dispatched his vice president, Joe Biden, to the Jewish state to reassure them that all was going well. Obama knew perfectly well that any treaty he might reach with Iran would require congressional ratification, a process in which Israel would have a powerful voice.

Israel had enjoyed congressional support since 1948, and that support had only grown stronger, reflecting the American people's support of Israel. While some attribute it to a well-funded pro-Israel lobbying effort, it is difficult to sway large numbers of congressmen with money if the position in question does not appeal to their constituents. As Israel became a more prosperous and powerful partner of the United States, Americans naturally gravitated toward it—just as they were naturally wary of Iran. Obama was right to be concerned that any deal that Israel did not support would have a rough road in Congress.

Having served in the Senate for thirty-seven years and visited Israel many times, Biden seemed a good choice for the mission. There was little progress to report, however, the Iranians having proved impervious to Obama's charm offensive during his first year in office. But Biden plowed ahead, repeating his standard story about meeting with Golda Meir during his first visit to the Jewish state before turning to Iran:

> From the moment we were elected, President Obama decided that we needed a new approach. He has sought to engage Iran's leaders for the purpose of changing their conduct, knowing full well how difficult that may be, but also knowing that if they fail to respond, we would be in a much stronger position to rally the international community to impose consequences for their actions.

While admitting that "Iran thus far has refused to cooperate" and was in fact increasing its nuclear activities, Biden insisted the plan was working. "You have to acknowledge that today Iran is more isolated with its own people as well as the region and in the world than it has been at any time in the past two decades."

The vice president then turned to the peace process with the Palestinians as a means to further isolate the Iranians, urging the Israelis to work toward a two-state solution. In President Abbas and Prime Minister Salam Fayyad, said Biden, "men who I've known for a long time, Israeli leaders finally have willing partners who share the goal of peace between two states and have the competence to establish a nation."[40] He urged that the Palestinian state be based on the 1967 borders with land swaps, condemned Israeli settlements in the West Bank, and departed.

Biden's intervention did nothing to allay Israeli trepidation over Obama's Iran policy, which only intensified over the next few years as the administration engaged in increasingly intense negotiations with Iran in Vienna. With justification, Israel prided itself for having taken concrete actions to prevent nuclear proliferation in the Middle East. Operation Opera had destroyed Saddam Hussein's nuclear reactor at Oskirk in 1981,[41] and Operation Outside the Box destroyed the Syrian reactor at Dair Azour in 2007.[42] Israeli leadership took a dim view of a diplomatic solution to the Iranian program. But even after an Iranian plot to murder then-Saudi Ambassador to the U.S. Adel al Jubir in a bomb attack on Café Milano in Georgetown was revealed in 2011, the Obama administration pressed on with their policy of conciliatory engagement with Iran.[43]

Obama himself traveled to Israel in 2013 to give what was described as "the most important speech ever made by an American leader" about resolving the Israel–Palestinian conflict.[44] After announcing that friends owed it to each other to be blunt and honest and equating the American civil-rights movement with the Book of Exodus, the president got down to brass tacks: Israel had to grant Palestinians statehood or the Jewish state's own democracy—not to mention its very future—would be called into question:

> You have the opportunity to be the generation that permanently secures the Zionist dream, or you can face a growing challenge to its future. Given the demographics west of the Jordan River, the only way for Israel to endure and thrive as a Jewish and democratic state is through the realization of an independent and viable Palestine. That is true.[45]

Given the centrality of a shared identity as democracies to the U.S.–Israel relationship, this was no idle threat. Obama went on to encourage Israelis to "put yourself into their [the Palestinians'] shoes." He insisted, as Biden had, that Abbas and Fayyad were reliable negotiating partners, and that "So many Palestinians—including young people—have rejected violence as a means of achieving their aspirations." The president once again concluded with his signature soaring rhetoric:

> And as a man who's been inspired in my own life by that timeless calling within the Jewish experience—*tikkun olam*—I am hopeful that we can draw upon what's best in ourselves to meet the challenges that will come; to win the battles for peace in the wake of so much war; and to do the work of repairing this world. That's your job. That's my job. That's the task of all of us.

The ensuing round of direct negotiations between Israel and the Palestinians initiated by Secretary Kerry and overseen by Special Envoy Martin Indyck foundered, however. In an attempt to revive them, the threat that if Israel did not comply with American demands for security concessions to the Palestinians to get to a deal the United States might no longer consider Israel a democracy was reiterated by Obama's new National Security Council Coordinator for the Middle East, Philip Gordon, who returned to Israel in July 2014. Gordon in fact took Obama's rhetoric a step further by warning that America would not be able to continue standing with Israel if no deal were made. While insisting the U.S. "has Israel's back," Gordon also noted,

> But in many of these realms, particularly outside the Security Council, our ability to contain the damage is limited, and becoming more and more challenging. This is what American friends of Israel mean when they express concerns about the potential for Israeli isolation if peace talks do not succeed.[46]

When Gordon made his remarks the relative calm that had held in Gaza when Obama visited Israel was rapidly disintegrating. But in their myopic focus on imposing a Palestinian state on Israel, the Obama administration continued to insist on concessions, even as the rockets began flying. Just months earlier, Palestinian Authority President Abbas announced a unity deal with Hamas in Gaza,[47] effectively killing the Obama round of the peace process and triggering the violence that would lead to an all-out war, but for the administration the burden was on Israel to reengage regardless.

In June 2014, three Jewish teenagers were abducted by the Iranian-proxy terrorist group Hamas while hitchhiking near the settlement of Kfar Etzion in the West Bank. Eyal Yifrach, nineteen, and Gil'ad Shaer and Naftali Frenkel, both sixteen, weren't soldiers, just some kids trying to get home.[48] The terrorists took them into the countryside and slaughtered them, making an audio recording of themselves singing joyfully as they killed them. Hamas kept the murders a secret, hoping to use a "hostage situation" to extort concessions from the Israeli government. The agonized families were strung along for weeks, hoping against hope that their sons would be returned alive. But then their bodies were found in a shallow grave near Hebron, and Hamas formally took responsibility for the attack.[49]

Prime Minister Netanyahu ordered an offensive know as Operation Protective Edge against Hamas in Gaza after the boys were recovered. Protective Edge went on for a month and a half, during which the IDF tried through airstrikes to degrade Hamas's ability to fire rockets into Israel. As it would do nine years later after the October 7 attacks, Hamas's propaganda arm tried to turn international opinion against Israel, applying pressure for a ceasefire as quickly as possible and the release of Hamas terrorists in Israeli prisons to resolve a conflict that Hamas itself had initiated.[50] It was successful.

It had become an imperative for the Obama administration to end the 2014 Gaza war, even if Hamas lived to fight another day as it was a serious problem going into the last year of negotiations for the nuclear deal. On the one hand, Hamas' murder of the three Israeli teens had been a gratuitous and deliberately provocative act of terrorist violence, and one of them, Naftali Frenkel, had had U.S. citizenship. But Iran, the main supporter of Hamas, wanted Operation Protective Edge to stop, and Obama was intent on getting a deal with Iran.[51] The administration was also trying to balance the competing Jewish and pro-Palestinian factions in its domestic political base. Secretary Kerry, for example, exercised his authority to slow-walk the provision of precision-guided munitions to Israel at the height of the conflict lest anyone think the United States was too robust in its support for the Jewish state.[52] Eventually the pressure became intolerable and Israel agreed to an uneasy peace, but one that came "with a sour taste of missed opportunity" to actually win the war in the words of Israel's Minister of Intelligence Yuval Steinitz.[53] The United States got what it wanted, however, and the nuclear negotiations continued.

The JCPOA

WHILE PRESIDENT OBAMA AT first thought the "Arab Spring" uprisings of 2011 (which he praised in his Israel speech) validated his new Middle East policy by bringing political liberalization to the region, the Israelis thought he was naïve. Destabilizing friendly despots like Hosni Mubarak of Egypt put them in danger.[54] In the aftermath, the personal relationship between the American president and the Israeli prime minister came under more strain than ever before in the history of the alliance. By 2013, the national security advisor Susan Rice was fuming that Netanyahu had done everything "but use the n-word" to describe Obama.[55] Another anonymous member of the Obama administration described Netanyahu as "chickens--t."[56] The staff sniping came to the surface during Netanyahu's visit to the White House in 2014, which was ostensibly to prepare for another round of negotiations with the Palestinians. Netanyahu, however, kept coming back to Iran, and Obama felt he had been "lectured" about his Middle East policy.[57]

An interim deal with Iran known as the Joint Plan of Action (JPOA) had been signed with the so-called "P5+1"—the five members of the Security Council (the United States, Russia, the United Kingdom, France, and China) and Germany in November 2013. This preliminary agreement provided for a six-month freeze in Iran's nuclear program in exchange for the relaxation of some of the economic sanctions that had been imposed on Iran by the Security Council, and it opened two more years of intense negotiations during Obama's second term.

In July 2015, after much cajoling and many concessions by the Americans and Europeans, a Joint Comprehensive Plan of Action (JCPOA) was adopted by the same P5+1 and Iran, but this time the agreement was coordinated by a representative of the European Union. It eventually was implemented in January 2016 as Obama entered his last year in office. The deal, as opaque as its bizarre name, was not formally ratified by any of the governments involved except Iran's, instead being put to a vote of the U.N. Security Council. No one at the head of state or ministerial level signed the JCPOA, and it was not binding by law on the participants.

An extraordinary deal for the Iranian regime, the JCPOA was quite different from what had been forecast by the Obama administration at the beginning of the negotiations. Gone were any references to Tehran's decades-long international sponsorship of terrorism, as well as any restrictions on its increasingly sophisticated and lethal missile programs. This meant that restrictions on the activities of the paramilitary forces that might use a nuclear weapon, as well as how they might deliver it, were omitted.

In addition, the issue of the Potential Military Dimension (PMD) of Iran's nuclear program was essentially punted. The term refers to ostensibly civilian nuclear activities that could also be used to develop a weapon, such as the extensive nuclear-research programs at Iranian universities with close ties to the IRGC, long suspected of having a military purpose. Subjecting these programs to inspection by the International Atomic Energy Agency (IAEA) would open them and their host institutions to international scrutiny. Iran flatly refused such inspections.

Desperate to get a deal, the head of the American delegation, John Kerry, eventually backed down. He was advised by a former member of Dennis Ross's negotiation team, Robert Malley, who had been a staunch advocate for the Palestinians during the Clinton-era negotiations. Now a member of Obama's NSC staff, Malley argued strongly that the Iranians were a potential regional force for good who could offset Israeli aggression if only the United States persuaded them that it was their friend. The resolution was that Iran and the IAEA would agree to a "roadmap" by which the IAEA would attest that the PMD of Iran's nuclear program largely ended in 2003 and would find no further activity going forward.[58]

A key concession to bringing Iran on board was sanctions relief. When Tehran proved unreceptive to the outreach that Obama had envisioned in Cairo, his administration worked through the United Nations to impose sweeping sanctions on Iran that substantially reduced exports of its economic lifeblood: oil. Despite exceptions for nations particularly reliant on Iran for energy—notably India, Japan, and South Korea, as well as China—the sanctions bit into Iran's economy. In addition, individual sanctions were placed on high-ranking Iranian military officers with links to terrorist activities, such as Qasem Soleimani, the head of the IRGC's elite Quds Force, who was coordinating Iran's regional activities in Lebanon, Syria, and Iraq.

Relief from these sanctions was the main incentive for Iran finally to engage in the nuclear negotiations. The original concept had been to keep the sanctions in place until Tehran made verified concessions of its own, but the mullahs would not budge until some money started flowing. Minor relief had accompanied the JPOA, but much more was expected from the JCPOA.

The Iranian team was skillfully led by the foreign minister, Javad Zarif, who had come into office with Iran's new president, Hassan Rouhani. Both Zarif and Rouhani were decades younger than the Supreme Leader, spoke excellent English, and had the reputation of being "reformers" who might be more willing to compromise than the hardliners in the regime. Zarif in particular developed a friendly rapport with Secretary Kerry and his team, along with the members of the Western media who eagerly met with him on his frequent trips to New York to visit the United Nations. In his roundtables with reporters, Zarif smoothly argued that Iran was eager for peace and for economic engagement with America and Europe. He would declare that the regime had no interest in a nuclear weapon and had never pursued one—in fact the Supreme Leader had some years previously declared a fatwa, or religious prohibition, against nuclear weapons—and the media dutifully reported that there was nothing to fear from Iran.[59]

While Zarif and Rouhani gave the regime smiling faces that appealed to Western audiences, their actions remained aggressive and provocative. After the JPOA talks concluded and while those for the JCPOA were gaining steam, Tehran appointed a new representative to its permanent mission at the United Nations. According to diplomatic protocol, along with heads of state of U.N. member nations, "PermReps," or ambassadors, enjoyed open-ended visas with unlimited entries into the United States and traditionally had no restrictions on their movements in America. Given the progress toward a nuclear deal, it might have been a moment for the regime to send a moderate, someone sympathetic to Rouhani and Zarif who would be a more affable representative in America.

Instead, Tehran nominated Hamid Aboutalebi, a member of the revolutionary old guard who had been involved in the hostage taking at the U.S. embassy in 1979. While he insisted that he had only been an interpreter, video footage and other evidence pointed to an active role in the attack. His appointment was in fact a deliberate insult to the United States and an indication of Iran's hostility. Secretary of State Kerry decided not to push back, asserting that he was obliged to issue the visa by the 1947 treaty that brought the United Nations headquarters to New York.[60]

Kerry's predecessor during the George H. W. Bush administration, George Shultz, had refused a one-time visa to Yasser Arafat in 1988 for his ties to terrorism, but the statute only listed espionage as the grounds to reject the application for an ambassador's visa. After Aboutalebi's appointment was announced and outrage grew among the American people who were not enthusiastic about having an embassy hostage taker living with impunity in New York City,[61] Congress intervened, led by Senator Ted Cruz of Texas, and amended the statute to list terrorism as well as espionage as activities that would automatically preclude obtaining such a visa.[62] Aboutalebi's application was withdrawn before a formal rejection could be issued, but the episode demonstrated that the regime's true intentions towards the United States were anything but friendly and that Congress at least recognized this reality.

The JCPOA was announced with great fanfare in the summer of 2015. The Iranians had driven a hard bargain. In return for accepting ten to fifteen years of restrictions on its civil nuclear program, including the Arak reactor and Fordow enrichment facility, as well as increased IAEA inspections, Iran was to be granted sweeping relief from the economic sanctions imposed by the United Nations, the United States, and the

European Union. At best, the JCPOA might put a hold on some aspects of Iran's nuclear program while preserving and legitimizing it and providing the regime with additional resources to expand it when the deal expired.[63]

The Obama administration took a victory lap. Secretary Kerry, in a press conference shortly after the deal was first unveiled, asserted that Iran's nuclear facilities would be repurposed for scientific research that would benefit humanity:

> Iran has also agreed to stop enriching uranium at its Fordow facility for the next 15 years. It will not even use or store fissile material on the site during that time. Instead, Fordow will be transformed into a nuclear, physics, and technology research center—it will be used, for example, to produce isotopes for cancer treatment, and it will be subject to daily inspection and it will have other nations working in unison with the Iranians within that technology center.[64]

In January 2016, when the IAEA certified that Iran had fulfilled the conditions of the JCPOA, President Obama celebrated the implementation of the agreement in a speech at the White House, smugly asserting that, thanks to his administration's skillful diplomacy, "Iran will not get its hands on a nuclear bomb."[65] He did not mention that as the implementation deadline had approached, Iran had started holding out for a better deal. In the end, the P5+1 had loaded four hundred million dollars in cash—euros and Swiss francs stacked on pallets—onto an unmarked cargo plane and sent the money to Iran.[66] Only when the cash arrived did Tehran finally release four American hostages, as it had agreed to do, and move on to implementation of the deal.

Despite the fanfare, the success of Obama's nuclear deal proved modest, doing little, in practical terms, to curb Iran's nuclear ambitions. If the regime had sufficient funds, it could still develop a weapon on its own over time through dual-use technologies or purchase one from a proliferator such as North Korea. To disguise these deficiencies, the

Obama administration had a clear and effective communications plan for the JCPOA developed by Ben Rhodes, the deputy national security advisor for strategic communications. Rhodes, who had done graduate work in fiction writing, had a talent for developing a persuasive narrative, which he fed to a willing audience of journalists to disseminate more broadly. The White House team was proud of its media mastery, and publicly boasted about the "echo chamber" it had established to sell the deal to the American people as a major triumph.[67]

Rhodes's fundamental message on the JCPOA was that it was the best deal that America could get and was therefore the only thing standing between the United States and nuclear war with Iran.[68] In his telling, there was simply no other choice, and concerns about Iran's terrorism, missile program, and PMD had to be sacrificed to get to this deal. He also argued that Israel should support the deal, since the Jewish state considered a nuclear-armed Iran an existential threat.

While it was certainly true that Israel considered the Islamic Republic armed with a nuclear weapon an existential threat, Israeli leaders had no confidence that this deal would prevent it from getting one. The Obama administration had hoped that diplomatic progress with Iran would also lead to a breakthrough on the stalled Israel–Palestinian peace process, but Israel faced other challenges from Iran that made it wary of the JCPOA, as well of a two-state solution.

For eight years, the Obama administration consistently and methodically tested its hypothesis that unconditional support for the U.S.–Israel alliance had failed and that America needed to seek new partners in the region—not just the Palestinians, but even more radically, Iran. As the president's second term neared its end, the American people remained conflicted about this approach. Their uncertainty was reflected in Congress, which passed the Iran Nuclear Agreement Review Act (INARA) in 2015 after the JCPOA deal was announced. Like the Iran deal itself, INARA lacked real teeth, but it did express bipartisan concerns about the nuclear deal and required the president to certify every ninety days that Iran was complying with its requirements.[69]

In a disturbing indication that Obama's charm offensive in the Middle East had not been as effective as hoped, a new radical-Islamic terrorist group burst onto the world stage as the JCPOA was being negotiated. The Islamic State in Iraq and Syria (ISIS) seemed to take the administration by surprise as it carried out a series of sensationally violent attacks and accomplished what Al-Qaeda never did: establishing its rule over a territory, or caliphate. Asked about ISIS in 2014, the president had responded dismissively:

> The analogy we use around here sometimes, and I think is accurate, is if a jayvee team puts on Lakers uniforms that doesn't make them Kobe Bryant. I think there is a distinction between the capacity and reach of a bin Laden and a network that is actively planning major terrorist plots against the homeland versus jihadists who are engaged in various local power struggles and disputes, often sectarian.
>
> Let's just keep in mind, Falluja is a profoundly conservative Sunni city in a country that, independent of anything we do, is deeply divided along sectarian lines. And how we think about terrorism has to be defined and specific enough that it doesn't lead us to think that any horrible actions that take place around the world that are motivated in part by an extremist Islamic ideology are a direct threat to us or something that we have to wade into.[70]

As ISIS made screaming headlines with ever more gruesome acts of terrorist violence, Obama's words seemed completely out of touch. The American journalists James Foley and Steven Sotloff were beheaded. The Jordanian pilot Moath al-Kasasbeh was burned to death in a cage. Twenty-one Egyptian Coptic Christians were beheaded on a beach in Libya. All the murders were carefully videoed and released on social media for maximum shock value.

ISIS also attacked in Europe and the United States. After fourteen Americans were killed in San Bernadino, California, in 2015 and another forty-nine in Orlando, Florida, in 2016, the president realized this was not just a regional Islamic issue and that the United States would need to return to Iraq in force to combat it. But the Iraq that American troops found in 2016 was different from the one they left when Obama declared the end of the war in 2011.[71] Not only was ISIS now an important presence, but Shiite militias that had mobilized after the Iraqi army failed to contain ISIS, known as the Popular Mobilization Forces (PMF), were also present on the battlefield.[72] The PMF had proved effective against ISIS, and the Obama strategy was to partner with them on the assumption that the enemy of my enemy can be my friend.

Unfortunately, while nominally Iraqi, the PMF in fact served another master: Iran. Under the direction of Qasem Soleimani, recently freed from U.S. sanctions under the terms of the JCPOA, the PMF were a de facto arm of the IRGC in Iraq.[73] Like Hezbollah in Lebanon and Hamas in Gaza, the PMF became powerful Iranian proxies both militarily and increasingly in the Iraqi government. While they were integrated into the grueling work of clearing territory from ISIS, they also started mounting attacks on American coalition forces and agitating for the complete withdrawal of the United States from Iraq.

To general surprise and even shock, Obama was not awarded with a "third term" when his former secretary of state Hillary Clinton lost the 2016 presidential election to Donald Trump. The new administration inherited a Middle East with an enriched Iran on the march, ISIS still entrenched in Iraq and Syria, and the U.S.–Israel alliance in its worst shape in more than two decades. While the president-elect had expressed general support for Israel and skepticism of the JCPOA on the campaign trail, his specific intents for the region were largely unknown when he took office on January 20, 2017.

CHAPTER FOUR:
WHAT'S NEXT?

The Trump Legacy

THE ELECTION OF Donald J. Trump to the U.S. presidency sent a seis-
mic shock through the international community. Virtually everyone
around the globe had assumed Hillary Clinton would be victorious, giving us a sort of hybrid Clinton-Obama term. Regardless of one's views
of either former president, that administration at least would have been
a known quantity.

Trump's election was nothing of the sort. A businessman and media
star who had never run for office before, Trump lacked the policy track
record that had come to be expected of a new American president. Nor
did he come with an army of long-term aides accustomed to dealing with
the career bureaucracy of the federal government, let alone the Congress.

As the world scrambled to get a sense of what the president-elect might
do, diplomats scurried around Washington trying to get a meeting with
anyone who might have some information they could send back to their
capitals. This strategic ambiguity proved beneficial for Trump, who was
unencumbered by the barnacles of conventional wisdom that restricted
the action of traditional politicians. With respect to the Middle East in
general and Israel in particular, this turned out to be a decisive advantage.

Trump had laid out a roadmap of his Middle East policy in March 2016
in a speech to the America-Israel Political Action Committee (AIPAC).
The invitation to address the group had, like almost everything else in
his first presidential campaign, stirred up considerable debate. Hillary
Clinton had addressed the group earlier in the week and had received a
warm reception, but on the grounds that Trump was conservative and

THE BATTLE FOR THE JEWISH STATE

therefore almost certainly antisemitic, some prominent members of the Jewish community condemned the invitation and threatened to walk out if he took the stage.[1]

Trump's AIPAC speech was in some ways remarkable for what he did not say. Gone was the routine lip service to a two-state solution based on the 1967 borders and the return of Palestinian refugees. Instead, he led with criticism of Obama's nuclear deal with Iran. After pointing out the many deficiencies of the JCPOA, Trump turned to the Islamic Republic's sponsorship of terrorism across the region and also in Gaza. He observed with characteristic bluntness that the United Nations was "not a friend" to either the United States or Israel, vowing to stand with Israel and condemning the antisemitic fanaticism in which the Palestinians were being indoctrinated. Then Trump got to the heart of what would be his Israel policy:

> But when the United States stands with Israel, the chances of peace really rise and rises exponentially. That's what will happen when Donald Trump is president of the United States. We will move the American embassy to the eternal capital of the Jewish people, Jerusalem. And we will send a clear signal that there is no daylight between America and our most reliable ally, the state of Israel. The Palestinians must come to the table knowing that the bond between the United States and Israel is absolutely, totally unbreakable.[2]

For anyone who cared to listen, the vision was there. Trump would end Obama's outreach to Iran and push back against its sponsorship of terrorism, stop attempts to establish a peace deal through the United Nations, and, most importantly, stand unequivocally with the Jewish state. And the first step would be to move the U.S. Embassy from Tel Aviv to Jerusalem. Trump received a standing ovation, no one walked out, and AIPAC issued an unprecedented apology to him for the criticism before the speech.[3]

Implementing the Jerusalem Recognition Act

AFTER THE 2016 ELECTION, former President Jimmy Carter published an opinion piece in *The New York Times* calling on the United States to unilaterally recognize a Palestinian state as a last-ditch attempt to save the Oslo process.[4] Carter, who had written the highly controversial book *Palestine: Peace Not Apartheid* in 2006 (which was so blatantly antisemitic that he later apologized to the Jewish community), represented the elite consensus that was reflexively hostile to Israel and sympathetic to the Palestinians. The incoming president, however, took a different tack, starting with the status of Jerusalem.

The Jewish, Christian, and Muslim faiths meet, mingle, and sometimes collide in Jerusalem, which also functions as the capital of Israel. Control of the holy city has been contested for millennia, and especially so since the foundation of modern Israel in 1948. When Israel became a state, it claimed Jerusalem as its capital, but large swaths of the city were controlled by other factions, and it has frequently been a flashpoint for violence.

The 1947 U.N. partition plan would have made Jerusalem a special zone administered by an international body and completely surrounded by Palestinian-controlled territories. On paper the plan sounded equitable, but in practice it proved completely unworkable. At the conclusion of the War of Independence in 1949, Israel took control of the western portion of the city and Jordan took control of the east, the division indicated on a map with a thick green pen—hence the term "green line."

This uneasy partition lasted until the 1967 war, when Israel conquered the entire city, placing it under Israeli law and making it the undivided capital of the Jewish state. The United States, following UNSCR 242, did not recognize Israeli control established through war despite the fact that Israel had won; it maintained its embassy in Tel Aviv and operated a consul-generalate in west Jerusalem to manage relations with the Palestinians in the West Bank and Gaza. Other countries, notably Russia, formally recognized east Jerusalem as the capital of a Palestinian state.

The dynamic between the U.S. embassy and consulate in Israel was unique and complicated. To prevent the Palestinians from feeling slighted, both the ambassador and the consul general had chief-of-mission status in the same country, leading to endless protocol and logistical complications. To start with, the consulate's location on Argon Road in Jerusalem was very much on the west side of the Green Line, meaning Palestinians had to go through Israeli checkpoints to get there and all the neighborhood around it was technically the purview of the ambassador. Attempts to establish a location in east Jerusalem or Ramallah were always frustrated by security concerns.

Bad blood between the two institutions festered, the consulate mandating, for example, that the passports of American babies born in the city indicate their birthplace as "Jerusalem," not "Israel." Despite a law enacted in 2002 to give U.S. citizens the option of indicating "Jerusalem, Israel," as the place of birth, Presidents Bush and Obama refused to enforce it on the grounds that it would be offensive to the Palestinians,[5] and it eventually fell to the Trump administration to resolve the issue in 2020 so that American passports could finally reflect the reality that Jerusalem is in Israel.[6]

Obama took his campaign to elevate the Palestinians to a new level in 2015 when he proposed hiring thirty-five armed guards trained in the West Bank to secure U.S. personnel traveling to and from the consulate into Palestinian areas. Needless to say, the idea of dozens of militarized Palestinians openly active in west Jerusalem under the aegis of the United States was a shock to the Israeli government, which strongly opposed the scheme. It also contradicted a 2011 security agreement between Israel and the United State that authorized only U.S. citizens and retired IDF soldiers working for the embassy to carry weapons in Israel. Backlash against the proposal was also swift in the United States, and it was scrapped after objections arose in Congress. Impracticable from the beginning, the proposal for armed Palestinian guards was another attempt by the Obama administration to endow the Palestinians with a status they did not actually have.

Congress had taken up the issue of Jerusalem's status in 1994 in an effort spearheaded by Senator Robert Dole, a future Republican candidate for president, and Congressman Newt Gingrich. The Republicans won control of the House of Representatives that fall. Gingrich, now Speaker of the House, prioritized the bill, and it passed with broad bipartisan support in October 1995. President Clinton signed the Jerusalem Recognition Act into law the following month.

The act had three main provisions. First and most important, it ended decades of U.S. ambiguity and recognized Jerusalem as the capital of Israel. Second, it exercised Congress's power of the purse by instructing the State Department to appropriate funds to move the American embassy from Tel Aviv to Jerusalem; if the embassy were not moved, funding for other U.S. embassies overseas would be cut in half, before being eliminated altogether.[7] But third, it included a national-security provision that allowed the president to waive the law for six months at a time if he judged that implementation would undermine the security of the United States.

For the next twenty-three years, four successive presidents—Clinton, Bush, Obama, and Trump—exercised that waiver every six months like clockwork. The rationale for the first three of those presidents was the same: the intelligence community assessed that moving the embassy could provoke another Arab attack on Israel, which could be overwhelmed and therefore did not really want the embassy moved. Furthermore, Clinton, Bush, and Obama believed that the Jerusalem Recognition Act threatened their years-long efforts to get to a Palestinian peace deal by unilaterally resolving a contentious issue they maintained should be settled through negotiations no matter how many times they failed.

Congress persisted as well, and every other year when a new Congress was sworn in, the Jerusalem Recognition Act would be passed again through both chambers. After Senator Dole retired, Senator Dean Heller led on the bill; he was joined by Senator Cruz in 2013 and by Senator Marco Rubio in 2015. Moving the embassy became a hot topic during the 2016 presidential primary, with all the major candidates vowing actually to do it, including Trump in his AIPAC address.

After President Trump took office in January 2017, the question became how to make this pledge a reality. The president took his campaign promises seriously and sought advice from a very different set of experts, all of whom were personally close to him and enjoyed his confidence. The embassy team was led by his son-in-law, Jared Kushner, the scion of a prominent New York real estate family and an observant Jew. He became a senior advisor to Trump, with an office in the West Wing close to the Oval Office. Kushner had married Trump's eldest daughter, Ivanka, in 2009 after she converted to Judaism. Their marriage contract was signed by one of Trump's top bankruptcy lawyers, David Friedman, whom the president nominated to be the American ambassador to Israel in the first days of the administration. The team was rounded out with Jason Greenblatt, a top corporate attorney in the Trump organization, who became the president's special envoy for the Middle East. While technically a State Department employee, Greenblatt sat in the Eisenhower Executive Office Building, with a sweeping view of the White House, and maintained close contact with Trump's National Security Council staff.

Kushner, Friedman, and Greenblatt managed the process of moving the embassy in partnership with the NSC. While the president technically could simply have issued an executive order his first day in office, he preferred to get Friedman on the ground in Israel to study the matter before he made the final decision. He even signed the waiver for the Jerusalem Recognition Act in June 2017 to ensure ample time for review and planning.

The State Department, led by Trump's first Secretary of State Rex Tillerson, was firmly opposed to the move. While unorthodox, the division of labor between the Tel Aviv embassy and the consulate general in Jerusalem was the status quo, each institution jealously guarding its turf. The intelligence community weighed in yet again with its well-established position that the action would trigger attacks on Israel, and on American assets in the region, and that Israel would not welcome the announcement.

Regardless of what it had communicated in the past, the Israeli government did not agree with this assessment in 2017. If the move could be done with the proper security, it would be welcomed.[8] Benjamin Netanyahu was still the prime minister, ably represented in Washington by Ambassador Ron Dermer, a former U.S. citizen who had renounced his citizenship in 2005 to become the economic attaché at the Israeli embassy in Washington.[9]

Hussein Agha, Robert Malley's coauthor of the Clinton peace process's postmortem, was then the PLO's representative in Washington, D.C. In his frequent visits to the White House, Agha, along with the ambassadors of a number of Arab capitals, lobbied furiously against the move. The situation, they warned, could rapidly get out of control and destroy any chance for a peace deal.

At first, events seemed to prove their point. Over the summer of 2017, tensions flared on Temple Mount in Jerusalem.[10] President Trump, encouraged by a congenial visit to the White House by President Mahmoud Abbas of the Palestinian Authority in May, had hoped he might be able to succeed where so many had failed, and plans for the "deal of the century" between Israel and the Palestinians were underway. But as the crisis in Jerusalem worsened, the Palestinians stopped communicating with the administration and even cut off all security cooperation with the Israelis.

President Abbas's predicament was obvious. On the one hand, he knew he needed ongoing engagement and, more importantly, funding from the United States to keep his regime going. On the other, he had a deeply radicalized population that had been raised on genocidal antisemitic hate, which he had been unwilling or unable to abate. His speech to the United Nations General Assembly in 2017 reflected that political reality, and as he had never been held to account for such radical rhetoric before, he assumed he would not be this time—especially with a Trump administration apparently eager to get to peace negotiations.

But there was another powerful dynamic at play in 2017—the fallout from the murder of Taylor Force, a U.S. Army combat veteran and Vanderbilt University business school student, by a Hamas terrorist in Tel Aviv in March of the previous year. The attacker was pursued and killed, winning for his family a sizable monthly pension from the Palestinian Authority's "Martyrs Fund." Outrage over the Palestinians' "pay to slay" policy led to the Taylor Force Act, which would incrementally cut U.S. funding for the Palestinians while they continued this practice.

Friedman was confirmed as ambassador in April 2017 and after about six months on the ground was ready to recommend a firm decision by the president to announce the embassy move. Asked how long the move would take, the State Department wanted a decade to select a site, study the security situation, and construct a new facility. Ambassador Friedman, however, understood that this demand was intended to delay the move until President Trump had left office. He responded that he could accomplish the move in five months by repurposing an existing U.S. facility in Jerusalem.[11]

After extensive consultations with regional leaders, including President Abbas, as well as careful security preparations in case the prophesied violence should break out, President Trump announced the move on December 6, 2017. Fortunately, there was no violence, but the establishment foreign-policy experts flooded the airways with predictions of disaster, first and foremost for the prospects of a deal between Israel and the Palestinians.

Aaron David Miller, who served in the State Department as a senior advisor on the Middle East peace process under Presidents George H. W. Bush, Bill Clinton, and George W. Bush, declared the issue of Jerusalem "too volatile to resolve now," predicting that the move was "likely to be far more trouble than it's worth—adding another layer of complication to a peace process that already faces long odds."[12] Paul Salem of the Middle East Institute warned the move would "dismantle American global leadership."[13] Dozens of musicians, actors, and authors decried the move in an open letter to the *Guardian* that reads like a Critical Race Theory textbook, concluding:

We reject Trump's collusion with such racist manipulation and his disregard for international law. We deplore his readiness to crown the Israeli military conquest of East Jerusalem and his indifference to Palestinian rights. As artists and as citizens, we challenge the ignorance and inhumanity of these policies, and celebrate the resilience of Palestinians living under occupation.[14]

Criticism hit a crescendo as Ambassador Friedman and his team closed in on their pledge to open the new U.S. embassy in Jerusalem on May 14, 2018—the seventieth anniversary of the foundation of modern Israel. During the festivities, liberal American news outlets broadcast "split screens" showing both the ceremony, attended by Prime Minister Netanyahu, Ambassador Friedman, and Jared and Ivanka Trump, and an eruption of Palestinian violence, apparently confirming the perils of the move.[15] But in reality, the violence was forty miles away in Gaza. Hamas incited the riots that would cost fifty-five Palestinians their lives to further the media narrative that Trump's embassy move would be a disaster. But the predicted pan-Arab attack on Israel did not materialize. Jerusalem itself remained calm, as did the rest of the region.

The Maximum Pressure Campaign

WHEN DONALD TRUMP BECAME president, the Obama-era JCPOA was entering its second year of implementation. Like moving the embassy, scrapping the nuclear deal with Iran was a campaign promise that President Trump could have accomplished by executive order on his first day in office, and some in his administration were urging just that. But once again, Trump decided to take some time to study the issue, especially after his first national security advisor, General Mike Flynn, was forced to resign after less than a month on the job, throwing his National Security Council into turmoil.

Flynn's successor, General H.R.McMaster, kept the NSC focused on orderly processes. In early April 2017, the question of recertifying Iran's compliance with the agreement and not sponsoring terrorism as required by the INARA legislation was handled according to standard NSC procedures, beginning with a meeting of a policy-coordinating committee. For the career bureaucrats involved, many of whom had participated in the JCPOA negotiations, this was a routine exercise that would result in the submission of a now-routine certification to Congress in short order. But for the political appointees, the suggestion that Donald Trump would certify that the Iranian regime was adhering to the JCPOA and not sponsoring terrorism came as a shock.

In the scramble that followed, stark divisions within the administration became clear. On the one hand, Secretary of State Rex Tillerson and Secretary of Defense James Mattis believed that the United States, having given its solemn word to abide by the agreement, should do so while exploring how to strengthen it. Secretary Mattis, in particular, insisted that the consequences of reneging would be serious. In his confirmation hearing, he had declared, "But when America gives her word, we have to live up to it."[16] Iran skeptics, however, thought the downside of staying in what Trump had called "the worst deal ever negotiated"[17] was greater, and in any case, no representative of the United States (or any other country for that matter) had signed the JCPOA, which was a product of the United Nations Security Council. But the author of *The Art of the Deal* wanted to try to get a better deal, so Trump agreed to the certification and gave the State Department six months to improve the JCPOA.

At the end of this period, no meaningful progress had been made. The Iranians, knowing that the original deal of 2015 was highly advantageous to them, had no interest in renegotiating harder terms for themselves. So in October 2017, President Trump took back the authority that Obama had ceded to the secretary of state and personally announced he could not issue the certification required by INARA. The United States would therefore formally cease compliance with the nuclear deal in May 2018.

President Trump's third national security advisor, John Bolton, an Iran hawk, organized what came to be known as the "Maximum Pressure Campaign" in coordination with colleagues from the State, Defense, and Treasury Departments. The concept was simple: the Iranian regime had spent almost every dollar it had received under the JCPOA on terrorism, missiles, and its nuclear program. If the resources were cut off, the regime would have to curtail these activities and, in time, negotiate a better deal if it wished to survive. Robert Greenway, then the director for Iran on the NSC, spearheaded the effort to produce an unsustainable trade imbalance for Iran while reducing its foreign-currency reserves. This process would in time cripple its economy and prevent it from funding not only its military and terrorism sectors, but also its nuclear program, and was fully coordinated with Israeli counterparts.

The Trump administration's concerns about Iran's malign intentions, particularly with respect to its nuclear program, were intensified by a visit from Prime Minister Netanyahu in April 2018. The Israeli delegation had unusual audio-visual requests for the briefing Netanyahu wanted to give to Trump, which caused a number of logistical challenges because of the nature of the equipment that could be used for the heads of state. But in the end, the prime minister was able to get his message clearly across: Israel's intelligence service, he revealed, had physically recovered an archive of material from Tehran detailing the history of Iran's nuclear program. From the outset it had included plans to construct nuclear weapons, plans that Iran never disclosed.[18] Here was proof that the JCPOA had been fraudulently negotiated, as the deal was based on Iran's assurances that their civil nuclear program had never had a military dimension. The archive contained, among other things, plans for nuclear weapons as well as two previously undisclosed nuclear sites.[19] Had Tehran been negotiating the nuclear deal in good faith, they could have revealed and surrendered this archive in 2015. Instead, they had meticulously—and secretly—maintained it.

Netanyahu's visit had increased concerns that Iran intended to pursue a nuclear weapon, posing an intolerable threat to both the United States and Israel. At the same time there were internal concerns in the Trump administration that reimposing sanctions on Iran's oil exports—then some 2.5 million barrels per day—would drive up energy prices in the United States. But during the period of the JCPOA, U.S. production had also increased substantially. Working with oil-producing nations that had swing capacity, such as Saudi Arabia and the United Arab Emirates, the United States was able to bridge the gap, and even when Iranian exports sank to four hundred thousand barrels per day in 2020, the projected spikes in oil prices did not occur.[20]

At the same time, Trump imposed additional unilateral sanctions on broad swaths of Iran's citizens and economy, including the financial and construction sectors.[21] For the first time, the United States sanctioned an element of a foreign military, designating the Islamic Republican Guard Corps as a foreign terrorist organization in 2019.[22] Naysayers predicted that Trump's approach would not be as effective as the U.N. sanctions imposed during Obama's presidency, which had brought Iran to the negotiating table for the JCPOA,[23] and dismissed the designation of the IRGC as symbolic at best.[24]

But events proved the naysayers wrong. Iran's fiscal condition was weak, and while the economic rewards from the nuclear deal, particularly from the lifting of the oil sanctions, had been considerable, they had been less than Tehran had hoped. Despite the active encouragement of the Obama administration, especially Secretary of State Kerry, for European investment in Iran, the response had been tepid. The money earned from oil exports was poured into military expenditures, not infrastructure or industrial investments that would lead to growth. And most countries, including China, were not willing to risk their ability to do business with the U.S. financial sector should sanctions return for the sake of comparatively minor deals with Iran. After growing more than 12 percent in 2016 following the implementation of the JCPOA, Iran's economy began to contract under the Trump sanctions, shrinking by 10 percent in 2019.[25] Unemployment rose as foreign-currency reserves dangerously dwindled, and the International Monetary Fund declared the Iranian economy in "extreme distress" because of the Maximum Pressure Campaign.[26]

Needless to say, Tehran did not accept the U.S. sanctions lying down, increasing regional attacks against American assets, particularly in Iraq,[27] and against commercial shipping through the Strait of Hormuz, one of the world's vital conduits of energy.[28]

In September 2019, Iran upped the ante with a complex drone and missile attack on Aramco's enormous oil refinery at Abqaiq, Saudi Arabia. With the capacity to produce some seven million barrels of gasoline, diesel, and jet fuel daily, the products that fuel the global economy, it is perhaps the most important energy installation on the planet.

The Iranian strikes caused massive fires at Abqaiq, forcing the refinery to shut down. At first, Iran's terrorist proxies, the Houthi in Yemen, claimed responsibility for the attacks, but both the Saudis and the United States were convinced they had originated in Iran itself. The drones and missiles were made in Iran, and a trajectory from Yemen could not be squared with the evidence. Abqaiq would be the first time Iran had directly attacked a neighbor since the Iran–Iraq War in the 1980s.[29]

By targeting civilian infrastructure, Iran sought to disrupt the world's energy markets, and at first it appeared their plan had been successful as the Saudis, with American assistance, worked to put the fires out and assess the damage. Fortunately, the destruction was not as severe as it had at first seemed, and Aramco brought the refinery back online in record time. The feared price spike failed to materialize.[30]

While this was a relief to the Trump administration, Iran clearly was escalating its regional attacks, and there would have to be an American response that would stop it, ideally without leading to a war. The options first presented to the president by the Pentagon were not satisfactory. Depending heavily on conventional methods, they carried with them the possibility of substantial civilian casualties. Iran's attack on the Abqaiq refinery, though potentially economically devastating, had been free of civilian injuries. President Trump—and the Saudis—were concerned that rather than ending the Iranian attacks, retaliation with bloodshed would provoke more of them.

Tensions rose when an Iranian strike killed an American contractor on a base in northern Iraq in December.[31] Large protests around the U.S. embassy in Baghdad followed. Shortly before Christmas, a plan materialized to target the IRGC leaders responsible for the strikes on American personnel and assets in the region. The kingpin was Qasem Soleimani, the head of the IRGC's elite Quds Force, who had been sanctioned for terrorism by the United States since 2007. That designation had been lifted under the terms of the JCPOA, but Trump had designated him as a terrorist again in 2018 when the United States ended its compliance with the nuclear deal. Soleimani earned the label, as he had been active in Iraq and Lebanon coordinating with Hezbollah and organizing PMF attacks on Americans. There were reports that he was organizing a larger action, possibly an attack on the U.S. embassy in Baghdad.[32]

Assured that the Department of Defense had both the intelligence and assets to carry out a targeted strike on Soleimani in Baghdad without collateral civilian casualties, President Trump did not hesitate. The action was carried out on January 3, 2020. A textbook operation, it showcased the United States' powerful and, to the Iranians, surprising capabilities. The president followed progress from his home at Mar-a-Lago, connected by a secure line to his senior aides in the White House Situation Room and the Department of Defense. The Chairman of the Joint Chiefs of Staff confirmed the strike, which also killed a key leader of the Iraqi PMF, Abu Mahdi al-Muhandas. Staff returned to their offices and monitored Twitter as other Iran watchers figured out what was happening in real time. Reports of the explosion quickly appeared, followed by claims from purported experts that it couldn't possibly have been Soleimani. Then the pictures were posted, including the famous image of one of his severed hands with its distinctive jeweled ring.

While many rejoiced at the elimination of a terrorist mastermind who had perpetuated so much violence in the Middle East and beyond, criticism also came swiftly. Think-tank denizens in Washington were suddenly deeply concerned about the process by which the president had made his decision, darkly predicting that the Iranians would be forced to escalate in retaliation.[33] But the Iranian response, when it came, was distinctly muted. Operation Martyr Soleimani included a ballistic missile attack on the Ain al-Asad airbase in western Iraq, which resulted in little real damage.[34] Deterrence appeared to have been restored as Trump entered the last year of his term.

From an Israeli perspective, the Maximum Pressure Campaign demonstrated the United States' commitment to countering, rather than appeasing, the Iranian threat in the Middle East, and Israel worked closely with the Trump administration to share intelligence and contribute to efforts such as terrorist-finance tracking. But the Israelis weren't the only ones to notice a new approach from Washington. Even before the attack on the Abqaiq refinery, the Maximum Pressure Campaign had led two Persian Gulf monarchies, the U.A.E., and Bahrain, to begin recalibrating their relations with Israel.

The Abraham Accords

ONE THING THAT PRESIDENT Trump had not mentioned in his AIPAC speech was the prospect of additional bilateral peace treaties between Israel and Muslim-majority countries along the lines of those with Egypt and Jordan. The conventional wisdom was that an agreement with the Palestinians had to come first. For its first three years, the Trump administration seemed to accept this. Kushner, with the support of Greenblatt (special envoy to the Middle East) and Ambassador Friedman, led the effort to put together a new approach to a deal, and in January 2020, shortly after the Soleimani strike, President Trump and Prime Minister Netanyahu unveiled the proposed terms at the White House.

The plan could have been a strong foundation for negotiations between Israel and the Palestinians,[35] and it was a serious offer by the Trump administration to draw upon the reservoir of trust it had built up with the Israelis to get to resolution. But the Palestinian Authority, which had also refused to engage after the president cut the UNRWA funding in 2017 and did not attend the preparatory 2019 "Peace to Prosperity" conference in Bahrain,[36] once again declined to engage.[37]

President Trump called the proffered deal the "last chance" for the Palestinians, and he turned out to be correct. Even as the U.A.E. and Bahraini ambassadors, Yousef Al Otaiba and Abdulla Al Khalifa, attended Trump's deal-of-the-century announcement at the White House, other diplomatic initiatives, which would overshadow any Israel–Palestinian deal, had quietly been underway for some months. The State and Defense Departments, supported by the National Security Council, had begun to host direct meetings between representatives of the U.A.E., Bahrain, and Israel in Washington.[38] By the end of the year, the process that would eventually become the Abraham Accords was beginning to take shape,[39] and negotiations proceeded even after the outbreak of COVID.

Once again, Kushner took the lead at the White House. The other participants in the confidential process were Secretary of State Mike Pompeo and his Special Envoy for Iran Brian Hook, Friedman (in Israel), the U.S. ambassador to the U.A.E., John Rakolta, Trump's fourth national security advisor, Robert O'Brien, as well as Robert Greenway and Miguel Correa on the NSC. Greenway, a retired Green Beret and intelligence professional, had been the chief NSC architect of the Maximum Pressure Campaign. Correa in particular played a critical role in gaining the trust of the U.A.E. While serving as defense attaché in Abu Dhabi in 2017, he personally intervened to rescue the Crown Prince Mohammed bin Zayed's son-in-law after a helicopter crash on a mission in Yemen.[40] In July 2020, Correa visited Sheik Mohammed in Abu Dhabi to seal the deal, which was announced two weeks later. Bahrain quickly came to an agreement as well, and both accords were signed at the White House on September 15, 2020. Morocco signed a similar agreement in December.

The Abraham Accords were modeled on the only successful agreements that had been reached since Israel's founding in that they were bilateral but with the participation of the U.S., but unlike Israel's peace deals with Egypt and Jordan, the Accords did not end a formal state of war. They rather were non-belligerence pacts that established formal diplomatic relations and opened the door to increased economic and social cooperation. The goal was thus not only increased regional security but also prosperity. The accords were bilateral, and each had its own particular provisions. The U.A.E. deal, for example, included concessions from Israel on annexation of parts of the West Bank while allowing the U.A.E. to purchase F-35 combat aircraft from the United States, a substantial upgrade for the defenses of a country on the front lines with Iran.[41] While Israel had previously opposed the sale on the grounds that it would threaten its qualitative military edge that had been established under President Reagan, with the assurances of peace from the U.A.E. this objection was dropped.

In exchange for Morocco's recognition of Israel, in an agreement drafted by Greenway in consultation with the U.S. ambassador to Rabat, David Fisher, the United States recognized the Kingdom's sovereignty over the disputed Western Sahara territory (a former Spanish colony). Though denounced by many on the left as a concession to colonialism,[42] the move simply acknowledged reality after thirty years of unsuccessful U.N.-sponsored negotiations between Morocco and the Polisario Front, a separatist radical armed group, had failed. The Polisario, originally formed in 1973 in opposition to Spanish rule, had turned their guns on Morocco when the Kingdom gained control of the area, were backed by Algeria and infiltrated by Iran, which was exploiting the Polisario to try to undermine King Mohammed VI's role as Commander of the Faithful to Morocco's Muslim-majority population. Morocco was a strong U.S. ally of long standing, while Algeria was closely aligned with Russia and China.[43] America's strategic interests clearly aligned with Morocco's, and recognition of Moroccan sovereignty over Western Sahara spared the region—and the Polisario—decades more of legal limbo.

As President Trump's first term came to a close, there were promising signs that the Accords could be expanded. An agreement with Kosovo, a Muslim-majority country in Europe, was negotiated. An agreement was also reached with Sudan, which would have brought badly needed stability to this breadbasket nation in sub-Saharan Africa if it had been implemented. The very concept of the Abraham Accords was unprecedented and the path forward uncertain. But Trump's novel policy approach made these agreements possible. The United States established a clear pro-Israel, anti-Iran posture in the region. The result was peace.

The success of the Abraham Accords came as a blow to the bipartisan Washington foreign-policy establishment, which had made a cottage industry out of the Israel–Palestinian peace process for more than three decades. Condemning Israeli settlements in the West Bank as an existential threat to negotiations, Secretary of State Kerry declared in 2016, "There will be no advanced and separate peace [for Israel] with the Arab world without the Palestinian process and Palestinian peace. Everybody needs to understand that."[44] But it turned out everybody who accepted Kerry's assumption was wrong—and the people who lost out were the Palestinians, who failed to grasp their last opportunity for a lasting deal before the Arabs decided they, the Palestinians, could no longer have a veto over progress in the Middle East.

The Biden-Harris Way: The Third Obama Term?

PRESIDENT TRUMP LOST THE White House in the 2020 election, and his successor, Joe Biden, moved quickly to reverse all his policies, even those that had been successful, including in the Middle East. From the status of the Palestinians to engaging with Iran to questioning the Abraham Accords, the Biden administration seemed determined to return to the Obama-era status quo. The cast of characters was largely the same, with Antony Blinken, Jake Sullivan, Robert Malley, and Philip Gordon—not to mention John Kerry—returning to senior appointments.

The first order of business was to restore the funding for the Palestinians that had been phased out during the Trump administration. The Biden administration started with $15 million in emergency COVID relief in March 2021.[45] This down payment was swiftly followed by larger sums, such as $235 million in April 2021 to fund UNRWA,[46] which President Biden proudly announced had ballooned into $316 million by July 2022.[47] By the end of 2023, the administration had provided more than $650 million to the Palestinians, with another $250 million requested for fiscal year 2024, although the Republican majority in the House managed to strip out this funding. All this money was supposedly intended to improve the Palestinians' quality of life, reducing violence and increasing the possibility of achieving the two-state solution to the conflict that Biden had long pursued.

Despite all this spending on the Palestinians, the October 7, 2023, attacks occurred. The contrast could not have been clearer. President Trump cut the funding to the Palestinians, and there were no mass-scale terrorist attacks. But when President Biden turned the spigot back on, the result was the worst terrorist attack in Israel's history.

Undeterred by this inconvenient truth, Biden directed hundreds of millions more to the Palestinians after October 7, even though the administration knew perfectly well that there was no way to ensure that the aid going into Gaza, for example, would not be siphoned off by Hamas.[48] In an emergency appropriation of funds for Ukraine, Israel, and Taiwan in May 2024, the administration included almost ten billion dollars—roughly double the amount given to the Palestinians since Oslo in the early 1990s—in undefined "humanitarian" funding, which could potentially be diverted to Gaza and the West Bank.[49]

The Biden administration had also prioritized renewed outreach to Iran from its earliest days in office, reversing the Maximum Pressure Campaign. To tempt the regime back to the negotiating table, the administration early on removed the Yemeni Houthi, an Iranian proxy, from its Foreign Terrorist Organization (FTO) and Specially Designated Global Terrorist (SDGT) lists.[50] While the move was characterized by Secretary of State Blinken as an effort to get humanitarian aid into the areas of Yemen controlled by the Houthi without incurring U.S. sanctions, it also made it easier for the Iranian regime to provide arms and other support to the Houthi.

After the Houthi were delisted, the Iranians agreed to join negotiations in Vienna for a new nuclear deal, but they refused to meet directly with the American delegation, communicating instead through European and Russian interlocutors. The process was predictably confused and inconclusive.[51] To sweeten the deal, the administration stopped enforcing the Trump-era unilateral sanctions on Iranian oil exports, which had fallen to a historically low level in 2020. By December 2022, Iran's exports had grown by more than a million barrels a day under President Biden.[52]

As it had during the Obama administration, the financial windfall was overwhelmingly spent on the Iranian military at home and sponsorship of terrorism abroad, the most spectacular example of which was the Hamas attack on Israel on October 7. While there were reports of distress from Iran's terrorist proxies during the Maximum Pressure Campaign,[53] under the Biden administration the regime had more funds at its disposal and more latitude in dispensing them through the region.

All Biden's concessions, however, had not resulted in any meaningful progress towards a new nuclear deal as his term drew to a close in 2024. The process was delt a significant blow the previous year when its main proponent in the administration, Malley, who served as special envoy for Iran, was suddenly suspended indefinitely without pay from the State Department. Investigative reporting later revealed that Malley's departure was related to his exposure to the Iran Experts Initiative, a network of Iranian ex-patriots sponsored by Tehran to influence public opinion in the United States.[54] Congress continues to demand information on Malley's reported leak of classified information to Iran's terrorist proxies.[55] None of this scandal, however, deterred Princeton University from inviting Malley to join its School of Public and International Affairs as a visiting professor, in a telling indicator of how America's elite academic institutions view such matters.[56]

Iran, meanwhile, was ratcheting up its sponsorship of terrorism across the Middle East. When President Trump came into office in 2017, the full scope of Iran's expanded terrorist activities became clear. In Iraq, the Shi'a militias—the PMF—with which Obama had tried to partner to defeat ISIS, turned out to be Iranian agents. After ISIS was decisively defeated and its caliphate dismantled on President Trump's orders at the beginning of his administration, the PMF's cooperation with American and allied forces quickly changed to hostility, and it became the main tool to attack U.S. assets in Iraq, which accelerated during the Biden administration. In the months following October 7, the PMF launched almost two hundred attacks on Americans, and it turned Iraq into what the Brookings Institution called an "Iranian client state."[57]

In Yemen, Biden's delisting of the Houthi as a terrorist group unfortunately did nothing to modify their terrorist behavior. In the weeks after the designation was lifted, they fired some forty missiles and rockets at civilian targets in Saudi Arabia.[58] A year later, they attacked the commercial airport in Abu Dhabi, killing three people.[59] After October 7, their attacks on shipping through the Red Sea became so disruptive that the State Department was forced to redesignate them as a SDGT although they were not put back on the more powerful FTO list.[60] Defensive U.S. and allied actions against them did not restore any sort of deterrence, and the attacks continued.

Hezbollah, Iran's oldest and most powerful proxy, turned out to be Hamas's key regional partner in the aftermath of October 7, creating a second front on Israel's northern border. Under persistent rocket and missile fire, some fifty thousand Israeli civilians were driven out of their homes, while tourism to the biblical sites around the Sea of Galilee was destroyed. But when asked on Air Force One on the trip home from Israel after the attacks if the United States would directly assist Israel in the event of a direct war with Hezbollah, Biden responded, "Not true."[61] Hezbollah's attacks have continued apace, even after the IDF eliminated, without U.S. knowledge or assistance, their terrorist mastermind Hassan Nasrallah on September 27, 2024.

The Biden-Harris administration also came into office determined to renounce the legacy of the Abraham Accords, at first even avoiding the use of the term altogether and opting for "normalization agreements" instead.[62] Support for strengthening them was at first tepid at best from a president who had referred to the next logical candidate for a deal, Saudi Arabia, as a state he would treat as a "pariah" during the 2020 campaign. But energy-market realities had changed Biden's tune, and he visited the Kingdom in 2022 and engaged directly with Crown Prince Mohammed bin Salman.[63] The foreign-policy disasters in Afghanistan and Ukraine left the administration hungry for a legacy achievement by the end of the term, and they decided that a new accord with Saudi Arabia would do.[64]

The Biden administration was correct to think that normalization of relations between Israel and Saudi Arabia would be a strong strategic gain for the United States in the Middle East and would be in the best interests of both Israel and Saudi Arabia. The president subsequently said he was so close to sealing the deal in September 2023 that Hamas's fears of peace sparked its October 7 attack, but in the waning days of Biden's presidency, prospects for a grand bargain, especially one including concessions for the Palestinians, dimmed.[65] Prime Minister Netanyahu then concluded that he was tabling the discussions until after the U.S. election.[66]

What's Next?

THE 2024 U.S. PRESIDENTIAL election presented an opportunity for the American people to compare the records in the Middle East of two very administrations—a contrast highlighted by the fourth anniversary of the signing of the Abraham Accords in September of that year and the first anniversary of the October 7 Hamas attack on Israel. While the issue is unlikely to turn a contest defined by economic and immigration issues, these two records, and their results, can be instructive for charting what comes next for American engagement in the Middle East. Even as China and the Pacific theater become a more pressing priority, the region will be critical to that conflict if only because of the energy resources it commands, which China needs, as well as its vital shipping lanes. At the moment, the United States is in essence providing security for China's energy imports as well as its exports to the European market at no cost to China primarily under the terms of the 1980 Carter Doctrine, which hardly makes sense today. So a recalibration is in order.

A 2024 essay in *Foreign Affairs* by Ben Rhodes, a deputy national security advisor for communications in the Obama administration, clearly presented the difference between President Trump's policy in the Middle East and the prevailing view among the Democrats. Rhodes disapproved, of course, of the former:

Trump pulled out of the Iran nuclear deal despite Iranian compliance, unshackling the country's nuclear program, escalating a proxy war across the Middle East, and sowing doubt across the world about whether the United States keeps its word. By moving the U.S. embassy in Israel from Tel Aviv to Jerusalem, recognizing the annexation of the Golan Heights, and pursuing the Abraham Accords, he cut the Palestinians out of Arab-Israeli normalization and emboldened Israel's far right, lighting a fuse that detonated in the current war.

He also had criticism for President Biden, who did not go far enough to reverse Trump's policies:

In the Middle East, the administration failed to move swiftly to reenter the politically contested Iran nuclear deal, opting instead to pursue what Biden called a "longer and stronger" agreement, even though Trump was the one who violated the deal's terms. Instead, the administration embraced Trump's Abraham Accords as central to its Middle East policy while reverting to confrontation with Iran. This effectively embraced Netanyahu's preferred course: a shift away from pursuing a two-state solution to the Israeli-Palestinian conflict and toward an open-ended proxy war with Tehran.[67]

In other words, Rhodes recommended a return to the Obama formula of unconditional engagement with Iran and open confrontation with Israel, particularly with regard to the legal standing of the Jewish state and the status of the Palestinians, while blaming the Abraham Accords for igniting the current conflict in Gaza.

There is, however, an alternative approach that would build on the policies of the first Trump term, which were themselves based on the Reagan-era initiatives that set the stage for what the U.S.–Israel alliance can become. In Jabotinsky's terms, this may well boil down to a "we win, they lose" formula. The immediate challenge would be to support Israel's clear victory over Hamas in Gaza by eliminating its remaining brigades and bringing Yahya Sinwar to justice in whatever form that takes. Given the IDF's progress, this could be achieved relatively quickly with clear American support. The signal to Egypt and Qatar should be that they are not negotiating a ceasefire, they are negotiating peace terms to include the immediate return of the remaining hostages. Israel's enemies from the Palestinians to Iran would then be on notice that the Jewish state is not going away for the simple reason that United States will not permit its eradication. However ironically, a clear defeat could be the one thing that would decisively shift the genocidal aspirations of the Palestinians revealed on October 7, and they might finally move on to negotiating "Plan B," which would be enormously in their best interests. An ambiguous end to the war, another "missed opportunity" to quote Minister Steinitz after the 2014 Gaza conflict, will only perpetuate the cycle of violence.

Once the Gaza war, as well as a looming conflict with Hezbollah in Lebanon, are resolved, there will be a wide range of possibilities to increase stability and prosperity in the Middle East. No American administration has yet approached the U.S.–Israel alliance strategically, so it has grown by fits and starts over the past seventy-five years, and peace has remained elusive. A new American administration could start by trying to eradicate the corrosive antisemitism that harms both Israel and the United States. Beyond that, simply returning to the policies that were successful in the Trump administration of 2017–21, while an improvement over the Biden-Harris approach, will not be sufficient to confront both the challenges—and opportunities—in the Middle East in 2025.

The easiest step would be to reimpose the funding freeze on the Palestinians, if for no other reason than the fact that the murderers of October 7 are being rewarded under the Palestinian "pay for slay" law in violation of the Taylor Force Act.[68] Furthermore, it has been credibly demonstrated that UNRWA employees were not only complicit but also active participants in those terrorist attacks.[69] The State Department Foreign Operations Appropriations Act for fiscal year 2024 prohibits any additional funding for UNRWA until March 2025, which is good as far as it goes,[70] but there should be a broader ban on any additional U.S.

funding for groups or entities that sponsor or participate in terrorist attacks on Israel.

In December 2020, President Trump signed the first formal Israel Strategy ever formulated by the U.S. government, a plan to develop and institutionalize the relationship. While this document was primarily concerned with security issues, it also addressed shared values and economic cooperation. Although discarded within weeks by the Biden administration, the plan is a foundation to build on by, for example, lengthening the term of the memoranda of understanding that outline the U.S.–Israel security partnership from ten years to twenty-five. The number of countries participating in the joint development of defensive weapons systems could be expanded to enable broader deployment. The existing U.S.–Israel Free Trade Agreement could be expanded. America could finally and unambiguously recognize Israel's sovereign borders.

To put together a regional alliance, the United States could build on the success of the Abraham Accords to achieve broader recognition of Israel. First and foremost, this means a deal with Saudi Arabia, the Middle East's largest and wealthiest Sunni monarchy, the home of the two holiest shrines in Islam, Mecca and Medina, and a strong U.S. ally for more than eighty years. Saudi recognition of Israel, a momentous step, would best be negotiated by a U.S. president who enjoyed the confidence of both sides, working with strong ambassadors, preferably political appointees, who have a clear line of communication with the White House. It would also be poetic justice to have the trajectory of U.S.–Israel security partnership that began with the 1981 Reagan administration MOU triggered by Israeli concerns about the sale of AWACS to Saudi Arabia to enter a new era with this momentous peace deal.

Any such agreement would require sustained engagement by the United States. If a security guarantee were included, it would have to be supported with a robust U.S. military posture in the region, which is already necessary to counter an increasingly belligerent China-backed Iran, especially in the Red Sea, where freedom of navigation must be restored.

If a U.S. security guarantee were a treaty obligation, it would require congressional approval. Such action would require, in turn, strong majorities in both houses in support of the policy. In addition, if the transfer of civil-nuclear technology or equipment between the United States and Saudi Arabia were contemplated, additional congressional action would be required in the form of a peaceful nuclear-cooperation agreement in accordance with Section 123 of the U.S. Atomic Energy Act. And if a "123 agreement" with Saudi Arabia differed substantially from those with other countries, supportive congressional majorities would be required.

All this work would be well worth it. The right Saudi Arabia–Israel agreement would unlock the possibility of the broader regional security and economic alliance originally proposed by President Trump on his first trip abroad in 2017, which began with a summit meeting with Arab states in Saudi Arabia as well as a visit to Israel—and included the first direct presidential flight from Riyadh to Tel Aviv.[71] The idea was not new, and there had been attempts to implement it before,[72] but a deal between Saudi Arabia and Israel would give a new urgency to the effort. The participants in the Riyadh Summit laid out the vision for the members of the Gulf Cooperation Council (Bahrain, Kuwait, Oman, Qatar, Saudi Arabia, U.A.E.), along with Egypt and Jordan, to join the United States in a Middle East Strategic Alliance (MESA). Quickly dubbed the "Arab NATO," MESA would in fact be much more than that, as it would include economic and political as well as military cooperation.[73]

But given the security situation in the Middle East today, military cooperation would be central to MESA's immediate mission, which would be confronting the threat from a nuclear-armed Iran. Iran has gone from 512 centrifuges producing uranium at weapons-grade enrichment when Biden was elected to almost ten thousand in 2024.[74] Secretary of State Antony Blinken publicly admitted that Iran is now one to two weeks from breakout when it decides to test a nuclear weapon.[75] The reality is that now there would not be time to reimpose the Maximum Pressure Campaign to starve the regime of the resources to get a weapon, as was the intent eight years ago, so it will be vitally important to quickly implement a credible military option that will deter Iran from trying. Getting

Israel into this planning with Gulf partners will be crucial to its success.

When MESA was first conceived, the inclusion of Israel was aspirational. By 2024, however, the successful integration of Israel into the U.S. Central Command security coordination under U.S. leadership has already started, and the Abraham Accords had begun to break down barriers to establishing MESA with Israel as a charter member. By extension, Morocco should also be considered for membership to anchor MESA's counterterrorism operations in Africa.

As a bloc of ten nations working in cooperation with the United States, MESA could be the model for other such regional alliances, which would build their own defensive and economic strength as American allies.[76] These free-market-driven, defensive agreements—leading not to subjugation but to mutual prosperity and security under American leadership—would be the U.S. answer to China's predatory and exploitative Belt and Road Initiative.

One such aspect of MESA that could be expanded through the Middle East and North Africa is energy cooperation.[77] Four members of the GCC—Kuwait, Qatar, Saudi Arabia, U.A.E.—are among the world's largest energy producers. But over the last two decades, they have been joined by the United States. Despite the restrictive and punitive environmental policies of the Biden-Harris administration, America produced a record amount of energy in 2023, 84 percent of it in the form of natural gas, oil, and coal.[78] Friendlier regulations, which would not only encourage increased production but also facilitate construction of the necessary infrastructure to support it, could make the United States a much larger energy exporter, giving it a major strategic advantage over adversaries such as China.

Although on a smaller scale, Israel has also moved from being intensely energy vulnerable to being an energy exporter thanks to the discovery of large natural gas fields under its territorial waters in the eastern Mediterranean.[79] These resources have fueled the conversion of Israel's coal-fired electricity generation plants to natural gas, leading to a substantial reduction in emissions as well as to energy security.[80]

Instead of scouring the world for reliable energy imports as they have had to do in the past, both the United States and Israel can work with fellow producers in MESA on a responsible energy policy, one that will keep global markets amply supplied to meet the world's burgeoning energy demands in coming years.[81] Existing organizations, such as the EMGF,[82] can be strengthened to support this effort that would now include the Gulf producers as well.

The benefits of this cooperation are already becoming clear. As the Abraham Accords were being negotiated in the summer of 2020, the usually separate spheres of energy markets and geopolitics collided when Chevron Corporation announced it was buying Noble Energy for five billion dollars, a deal that contributed as much to establishing a sustainable peace in the Middle East as do the Abraham Accords themselves.[83] Chevron has long been an American titan in the energy-rich Middle East, first discovering oil in Bahrain in 1932. The company now operates in the Partitioned Zone between Kuwait and Saudi Arabia in partnership with both countries, with whom Chevron enjoys enormously lucrative and historic relationships.

Noble on the other hand is a relatively new and small operator, whose primary regional focus has been on developing natural-gas resources in the eastern Mediterranean. Important partners include Egypt, whose Leviathan gas field has been of interest to Chevron for some time. But Noble also does significant work with Israel's Delek Drilling, L.P.[84] For decades, conventional wisdom has held that if a company's bread-and-butter business is in the Arab countries of the Persian Gulf, the danger of new conflicts or boycotts makes it prudent to avoid exposure to Israel. This should have prohibited Chevron's purchase of Noble.

But conventional wisdom no longer holds. Chevron's new Israel page on its website demonstrates there is no effort to mask the connection to the Jewish state through its Noble subsidiary.[85] Noble has been renamed Chevron Mediterranean Limited, and its "Who We Are" website page prominently features a photograph of a natural-gas barge proudly flying an Israeli flag. In the absence of ironclad assurances from the

Gulf states, including Saudi Arabia, that this activity would in no way threaten Chevron's larger business in the region, this deal would not have been possible. Progress in the energy industry thus suggests that there is an appetite for expanding this cooperation further under more forward-leaning U.S. leadership.[86] There is even the possibility that the Palestinians, who participate in the EMGF, might one day have a share in this success with the development of the Gaza Marine gas field.

In the wake of October 7, however, all these good prospects in the Middle East will mean nothing if antisemitism continues to grow unchecked here at home in America. It is clearly not enough simply to have a president who is pro-Israel and not antisemitic. The United States needs an unambiguous policy to eradicate the bigotry that leaders from Jimmy Carter to Kamala Harris have permitted, a bigotry funded by a combination of global elites and the Iranian regime. American antisemitism isn't just hatred of Jews, it is hatred of the very essence of the United States as well. An unambiguous statement by the commander in chief that antisemitism is a cancer on American society could lay the groundwork for a concrete policy to fight it.

While the State Department has a special envoy to combat antisemitism, this envoy's activities have been international, not domestic. As Trump's deputy special envoy for antisemitism Ellie Cohanim argued before October 7, this office should be transferred to the White House to demonstrate a Presidential commitment to a broader mandate:

> Within the Executive Office of the President of the United States, there should be an Office to Combat Domestic Anti-Semitism, led by the domestic anti-Semitism czar. This senior official should be given the authority and responsibility to coordinate a whole-of-government approach to dealing with domestic Jew-hatred. Such an effort would include bringing together the resources of the FBI, Department of Justice, Department of Education, Department of Homeland Security and the FCC.[87]

The extent and intensity of antisemitism in the United States after October 7, 2023, gave this proposal a new urgency. It became clear that while antisemitism across the political spectrum in all its forms is an evil that should be countered, the bulk of antisemitic activity in America is carried out by pro-Palestinian and pro-Hamas networks that were waiting for a spectacular attack in the Middle East to bring the battle to the United States.

The statistics are chilling. During Trump's term in office, antisemitic attacks in America held steady at around two thousand per year. In 2021, they rose to 2,717, then to 3,697 in 2022. But in just the three months after October 7, there were 3,291. If these trends hold, the United States could see more than twelve thousand antisemitic attacks—an increase of more than 300 percent—in the year after the most consequential attack on Jews since World War II. For comparison, Islamophobic incidents also rose in the United States in 2023, but by 56 percent.[88]

Antisemitism is beyond a problem. It is an epidemic targeting younger Americans, many of whom spend much of their time on college campuses, where this hateful ideology is prevalent. When the Anti-Defamation League started tracking American antisemitism in the 1960s, the problem was more common among the older population than among the young, a disparity that encouraged the assumption that hatred of Jews would dwindle with time. But now that favorable trend has been reversed. Younger Americans are more than twice as likely to hold antisemitic views than their older counterparts. The problem will only metastasize if left unchecked.[89]

The spread of antisemitism is no accident but part of a plan of some years' duration to make this prejudice acceptable in the United States. The desired outcome is not only the severing of the U.S.–Israel alliance but also a fundamental change of national allegiance away from traditional Judeo-Christian values. To enact the plan, its proponents have taken advantage of the institutions of America's free society, from academia to the media to the democratic process.

The most visible expressions of antisemitism since October 7 have come from the pro-Hamas networks active in American cities and universities, and they should be the first targets. Under the terms of the Antiterrorism and Effective Death Penalty Act of 1996 (AEDPA), those who have promoted and lent political legitimacy to Hamas have provided material support to a designated foreign terrorist group, regardless of where this support takes place. Congress should amend and strengthen AEDPA to counter the threats America faces today, especially the networks through which these organizations are funded.[90] Institutions that harbor and support terrorist groups, notably colleges and universities, should also forfeit their federal and state funding.

There is an important precedent for such an effort: the 2008 trial and conviction of the Holy Land Foundation for Relief and Development (HLF) and its leadership for providing material support for Hamas. Based in a Dallas suburb and once the largest Muslim charity in the United States, HLF existed to funnel resources to Hamas and to promote the group's image in America.[91] Once HLF was closed and its senior leadership imprisoned, other sources of support dried up for a period, but they were clearly not eradicated as recent activities demonstrate. Much work remains to be done.

The appointment of a presidential czar for antisemitism who would be in charge of coordinating the campaign against the noxious pro-Hamas manifestation of antisemitism with the Department of Justice would send a clear message that such views are not only bigoted and abhorrent but can also bring significant legal penalties. These penalties could go a long way towards eradicating the permissive atmosphere that has fostered the mainstreaming of antisemitism in the United States, as revealed by recent events such as the Congressional testimony by the Presidents of Harvard, MIT, and Penn discussed by Senator Cruz in his foreword to this book.

Doing so would discourage the spread of antisemitism in America before it becomes what history teaches can be a deadly, culture-wide threat. Imagine if Albert Einstein, instead of leaving Germany in 1932, had enjoyed the support of gentile allies who stood up to the Nazi death machine before it became operational. Einstein did not find those allies, however, and had to flee to an America that already had its own antisemitism problem. He was one of the lucky ones. After the Holocaust, the modern state of Israel became a necessity for the preservation of the Jewish people, and over the next seven decades the United States has become an increasingly important partner in this project that now must confront the danger that is growing in its own society.

Since October 7, 2023, two distinct camps have emerged in America, revealing a divide in support for Israel. One side believes that the United States has backed the wrong horse. An oppressive and illegitimate Israel, they claim, is what ails the modern Middle East, and support for the Jewish state prevents the United States for truly atoning for its racist and imperialist past. The other camp believes that the survival of Israel is critically important to both the security and culture of the United States, and that the reasons many of America's founding fathers were Zionists remain valid today. Jews, then, are essential participants in the American experiment, which will celebrate its two hundred fiftieth anniversary in 2026.

Conclusion

THE PURPOSE OF THIS book is to explain why the pro-Israel side is correct and to chart a safe course at a moment when the U.S.–Israel alliance hangs in the balance. Regardless of who wins the 2024 election, the good news is that the pro-Israel side still comprises a significant majority of Americans, but, with the balance shifting among the younger demographic, we cannot assume that it will prevail without concerted effort against an increasingly aggressive threat.[92] *The Atlantic* recently published a chilling article titled "The United States and Israel Are Coming Apart" that argues,

> A rift has opened between Israel and the United States. No breach between the two countries has been as wide or as deep since the mid-1950s, when the Eisenhower administration

compelled Israel to withdraw from the Sinai Peninsula. President Joe Biden expressed grave displeasure with Israel this week over the strike that killed seven aid workers from World Central Kitchen, and a phone call between him and Israeli Prime Minister Benjamin Netanyahu yesterday was reportedly tense. But those are just the surface-level fissures that emanate from a much more profound split.

Washington and Jerusalem don't just differ over tactics, nor even just over plans for the medium term. For the first time in modern memory, the two countries are also at odds over long-term visions and goals, as Israel's territorial ambitions are coming into ever-greater and more direct conflict with U.S. strategic interests in the Middle East.[93]

The same magazine did publish a strikingly similar piece a decade ago at the end of the Obama administration,[94] and that documentation of the demise of the U.S.–Israel alliance turned out to be much exaggerated. But we cannot simply assume this is once again the case in 2024. Now viewed with some historical perspective, the choice between a successful if unorthodox approach to the Middle East under President Trump and the decades of bipartisan failure most recently manifested in the Biden-Harris administration could not be more stark.

We might simply look at the actions of our mutual adversaries, as Iran is not only attacking Israel in the Middle East but is also attempting to meddle in the U.S. election—and even potting to assassinate former President Trump to prevent his reelection. We are stronger together than apart.

Ze'ev Jabotinsky got it right more than a century ago when he argued that the defenses of a Jewish state had to be an impenetrable iron wall, a wall that can now be manifested in the U.S.–Israel alliance. That is why actually winning the war against Israel—which is also a war against the United States—that broke out afresh on October 7 is so critically important not only to our two countries, but also to the rest of the civilized world.

ENDNOTES

Chapter One

1   Matthew Mpoke Bigg, "What We Know About Iran's Attack on Israel and What Happens Next," *The New York Times*, April 14, 2024, https://www.nytimes.com/2024/04/14/world/middleeast/iran-israel-drones-attack.html.

2   Shibley Telhami, "After Abbas-Trump meeting: Is Abbas' optimism justified?," Brookings, May 5, 2017, https://www.brookings.edu/articles/after-abbas-trump-meeting-is-abbas-optimism-justified/.

3   "FULL TEXT: Palestinian President Mahmoud Abbas' Address to UN General Assembly," *Haaretz*, September 20, 2017, https://www.haaretz.com/middle-east-news/palestinians/2017-09-20/ty-article/full-text-abbas-address-to-un-general-assembly/0000017f-e0d5-df7c-a5ff-e2ff8a290000.

4   President Donald J. Trump, "Statement by President Trump on Jerusalem," December 6, 2017, https://trumpwhitehouse.archives.gov/briefings-statements/statement-president-trump-jerusalem/.

5   TOI Staff, "Bahrain leader condemns Hamas Oct. 7 onslaught, calls for release of hostages," *The Times of Israel*, November 20, 2023, https://www.timesofisrael.com/bahrain-leader-condemns-hamas-oct-7-onslaught-calls-for-release-of-hostages/.

6   Gal Beckerman, "'The Middle East Region Is Quieter Today Than It Has Been in Two Decades,'" *The Atlantic*, October 7, 2023, https://www.theatlantic.com/international/archive/2023/10/israel-war-middle-east-jake-sullivan/675580/.

7   Patrick Kingsley, Aaron Boxerman, and Hiba Yazbek, "Hundreds Reported Killed in Blast at a Gaza Hospital," *The New York Times*, October 17, 2023, https://www.nytimes.com/2023/10/17/world/middleeast/gaza-hospital-explosion-israel.html.

8   Katie Robertson, "After Hospital Blast, Headlines Shift With Changing Claims," *The New York Times*, October 18, 2023, https://www.nytimes.com/2023/10/18/business/media/hospital-blast-gaza-reports.html.

9   President Joseph R. Biden, "Remarks by President Biden on the October 7th Ter-
     rorist Attacks and the Resilience of the State of Israel and its People," October 18,
     2023, https://www.whitehouse.gov/briefing-room/speeches-remarks/2023/10/18/
     remarks-by-president-biden-on-the-october-7th-terrorist-attacks-and-the-resil-
     ience-of-the-state-of-israel-and-its-people-tel-aviv-israel/.

10   Brett Samuels, "Biden warns Israel not to repeat mistakes of US response after
     9/11," *The Hill*, October 18, 2013, https://thehill.com/homenews/administra-
     tion/4262626-biden-warns-israel-mistakes-after-9-11/.

11   Donald Rumsfeld, *Known and Unknown: A Memoir* (New York: Sentinel, 2011),
     352–58.

12   Adam Kredo, "Biden Admin Deletes Tweet Instructing Israel to Stand Down
     Amid Hamas Terror," *The Washington Free Beacon*, October 7, 2023, https://free-
     beacon.com/biden-administration/biden-admin-deletes-tweet-instructing-isra-
     el-to-stand-down-amid-hamas-terror/. See also remarks by Senator Ted Cruz in
     Congress on October 18, 2023: U.S. Congress, *Congressional Record* vol. 169, no.
     171, 118th Cong., 1st sess., October 18, 2023, https://www.congress.gov/congres-
     sional-record/volume-169/issue-171/senate-section/article/S5080-1.

13   Benjamin Wallace-Wells, "Why a State Department Official Lost Hope in Israel,"
     The New Yorker, November 6, 2023, https://www.newyorker.com/news/the-politi-
     cal-scene/why-a-state-department-official-lost-hope-in-israel.

14   Victoria Coates and Jamie Metzl, "White House staffers protesting Biden should
     be fired," *The Hill*, December 31, 2023, thehill.com/opinion/white-house/4379866-
     white-house-staffers-protesting-biden-should-be-fired/.

15   Maria Abi-Habib, Michael Crowley, and Edward Wong, "More Than 500 U.S. Of-
     ficials Sign Letter Protesting Biden's Israel Policy," *The New York Times*, November
     14, 2023, https://www.nytimes.com/2023/11/14/us/politics/israel-biden-letter-ga-
     za-cease-fire.html.

16   Jonathan Guyer, "'Extraordinary': Biden administration staffers' growing dissent
     against Gaza policy," *The Guardian*, January 6, 2024, https://www.theguardian.
     com/us-news/2024/jan/06/biden-administration-staff-gaza-policy-protest.

17   Camila DeChalus, "Biden administration staffers call for ceasefire at vigil outside
     White House," CNN, December 13, 2023, https://edition.cnn.com/2023/12/13/
     politics/biden-staffers-ceasefire-vigil-white-house/.

18 "U.S. federal employees plan walkout in protest of Biden's Israel policy," *i24 News*, January 16, 2024, https://www.i24news.tv/en/news/international/americas/1705440514-u-s-federal-employees-plan-walkout-in-protest-of-biden-s-israel-policy.

19 Mike Gonzalez and Katharine Cornell Gorka, *NextGen Marxism: What It Is and How to Combat It* (New York: Encounter Books, 2024), 12.

20 "Luxns Military Shemagh Tactical Desert Scarf / 100% Cotton Keffiyeh Scarf Wrap for Men And Women," Amazon.com, https://www.amazon.com/Military-Shemagh-Tactical-Desert-Keffiyeh/dp/Bo8ZRW1RKY/ref=asc_df_Bo8ZRW1RKY?tag=bingshoppinga-20&linkCode=dfo&hvadid=79852147245096&hvnetw=o&hvqmt=e&hvbmt=be&hvdev=c&hvlocint=&hvlocphy=&hvtargid=pla-4583451675762964&psc=1 (accessed August 22, 2024).

21 Victoria Coates and Chip Roy, "Kamala Harris and the Truth about Israel," *Newsweek*, October 5, 2021, https://www.newsweek.com/kamala-harris-truth-about-israel-opinion-1635388.

22 Noura Erakat, Darryl Li, and John Reynolds, "Race, Palestine, and International Law," *AJIL Unbound* 117 (2023): 77–81, https://doi.org/10.1017/aju.2023.9.

23 Besheer Mohamed, "New estimates show U.S. Muslim population continues to grow," Pew Research Institute, January 3, 2018, https://www.pewresearch.org/short-reads/2018/01/03/new-estimates-show-u-s-muslim-population-continues-to-grow/.

24 Lili Pike, "Why so many young people showed up on Election Day," *Vox*, November 7, 2020, https://www.vox.com/2020/11/7/21552248/youth-vote-2020-georgia-biden-covid-19-racism-climate-change.

25 Isabel Kershner, "Facing Global Outrage, Netanyahu Calls Civilian Deaths in Rafah Strike 'Tragic Accident'," *The New York Times*, May 27, 2024, https://www.nytimes.com/2024/05/27/world/middleeast/israel-rafah-civilian-deaths.html.

26 "Doctrine of Hamas," Wilson Center, October 20, 2023, https://www.wilsoncenter.org/article/doctrine-hamas.

27 "President Bush's Second Inaugural Address," NPR, January 20, 2005, https://www.npr.org/2005/01/20/4460172/president-bushs-second-inaugural-address.

28 Ted Cruz, "A Tale of two hospitals: One in Israel, one in Gaza," *The Washington Times*, July 30, 2014, https://www.washingtontimes.com/news/2014/jul/30/cruz-a-tale-of-two-hospitals/.

29 CJ Staff, "UNC faculty to withhold final grades for all until suspended protesters are re-instated," *The Carolina Journal*, May 6, 2024, https://www.carolinajournal.com/unc-faculty-to-withhold-final-grades-for-all-until-suspended-protesters-are-re-instated/.

30 *Students for Fair Admissions, Inc. v. President and Fellows of Harvard College*, 600 U.S. ___ (2023) and *Students for Fair Admissions, Inc. v. University of North Carolina*, 567 F. Supp. 3d 580 (M.D.N.C. 2021).

31 Alex Kasprak, "Fact Check: A George Washington Statue at GWU Was Allegedly Defaced by Pro-Palestinian Protesters. Here's the Evidence," Snopes, May 3, 2024, https://www.snopes.com/fact-check/washington-statue-defaced-gwu/.

32 Vivian Salama, "Blinken Says He *Sees* His Own Children in Faces of Injured Palestinian Boys and Girls," *The Wall Street Journal*, November 6, 2023, https://www.wsj.com/livecoverage/israel-hamas-war-gaza-strip-2023-11-04/card/blinken-says-he-sees-his-own-children-in-faces-of-injured-palestinian-boys-and-girls-mtMFpzKWavYjLgQyzhlJ.

33 Golda Meir, *A Land of Our Own: An Oral Autobiography* (Ann Arbor: The University of Michigan Press, 1973), 242.

34 Mared Gwyn Jones, "UNRWA chief has no intention to resign over allegations, hopes EU will continue funding," Euronews, February 12, 2024, https://www.euronews.com/my-europe/2024/02/12/unrwa-chief-has-no-intention-to-resign-over-allegations-hopes-eu-will-continue-funding.

35 President Joe Biden, "2024 State of the Union," March 7, 2024, https://www.whitehouse.gov/state-of-the-union-2024/.

36 Haley Britzky, Natasha Bertrand, and Oren Liebermann, "Pentagon says none of the aid unloaded from US pier off coast of Gaza has been delivered to broader Palestinian population," CNN, May 21, 2024, https://www.cnn.com/2024/05/21/politics/us-gaza-pier-aid-not-delivered/index.html.

37 Courtney Kube, "Pentagon to shut down its troubled Gaza pier aid operation," NBC News, July 12, 2024, https://www.nbcnews.com/investigations/pentagon-shut-troubled-gaza-pier-aid-operation-rcna161646.

38 Jeremy Sharon, "UN cuts by more than half the number of women, children 'identified' as killed in Gaza," *The Times of Israel*, May 13, 2024, https://www.timesofisrael.com/un-drastically-revises-downward-number-of-identified-women-children-killed-in-gaza/.

39   President Joe Biden, "Remarks by President Biden on the Release of Hostages from Gaza," November 24, 2023, https://www.whitehouse.gov/briefing-room/speeches-remarks/2023/11/24/remarks-by-president-biden-on-the-release-of-hostages-from-gaza/.

40   President Joe Biden, "Remarks by President Biden at the Morehouse College Class of 2024 Commencement Address," May 19, 2024, https://www.whitehouse.gov/briefing-room/speeches-remarks/2024/05/19/remarks-by-president-biden-at-the-morehouse-college-class-of-2024-commencement-address-atlanta-ga/#:~:text=I%20don%27t%20know%20any,Morehouse%20education%20makes%20you%20fearless.

41   Reuters and TOI Staff, "Hostage Noa Argamani rescued in time to see her terminally ill mother," *The Times of Israel*, June 9, 2024, https://www.timesofisrael.com/hamas-hostage-noa-argamani-rescued-in-time-to-see-her-terminally-ill-mother/.

42   Anders Hagstrom, "Kamala Harris mourns death of Palestinians in raid that rescued 4 Israeli hostages," Fox News, https://www.foxnews.com/politics/kamala-harris-mourns-death-palestinians-raid-rescued-4-israeli-hostages.

43   Steven Nelson, "Biden calls Netanyahu 'my friend for decades' as Israeli PM regains power," *New York Post*, December 29, 2022, https://nypost.com/2022/12/29/biden-calls-netanyahu-my-friend-for-decades-as-israeli-pm-regains-power/.

44   Matthew Lee, "Biden administration restores Trump-rescinded policy on illegitimacy of Israeli settlements," Associated Press, https://apnews.com/article/israel-settlements-illegitimate-palestine-biden-rescind-law-0bed7cf5d-6f98012193e9f5075eb719a.

45   Karin Laub, "Palestinian poll shows a rise in Hamas support and close to 90% wanting US-backed Abbas to resign," Associated Press, https://apnews.com/article/israel-hamas-palestinians-opinion-poll-wartime-views-a0baade915619cd070b-5393844bc4514.

46   "Harris: It's important to distinguish between Israeli people and government," *The Times of Israel*, March 9, 2024, https://www.timesofisrael.com/liveblog_entry/harris-its-important-to-distinguish-between-israeli-people-and-government/.

47   TOI Staff, "Full text of Senator Chuck Schumer's speech: 'Israeli elections are the only way,'" *The Times of Israel*, March 15, 2024, https://www.timesofisrael.com/full-text-of-senator-chuck-schumers-speech-israeli-elections-are-the-only-way/.

48   United Nations Security Council, "Resolution 2728: The situation in the Middle East, including the Palestinian question," March 25, 2024, https://documents.un.org/doc/undoc/gen/n24/080/81/pdf/n2408081.pdf.

49 Rep. Chip Roy and Victoria Coates, "Biden's moral equivalency between Israel and the Palestinians will result in failure—again," Fox News, April 16, 2024, https://www.foxnews.com/opinion/bidens-moral-equivalency-between-israel-palestinians-will-result-failure-again.

50 Ambassador Robert Wood, "Explanation of Vote Delivered at the UN General Assembly Emergency Special Session on the Palestinian UN Membership Resolution," United States Mission to the United Nations, May 10, 2024, https://usun.usmission.gov/explanation-of-vote-delivered-at-the-un-general-assembly-emergency-special-session-on-the-palestinian-un-membership-resolution/. 51

51 Karim A. A. Khan, "Statement of ICC Prosecutor Karim A.A. Khan KC: Applications for arrest warrants in the situation in the State of Palestine," International Criminal Court, May 20, 2024, https://www.icc-cpi.int/news/statement-icc-prosecutor-karim-aa-khan-kc-applications-arrest-warrants-situation-state.

52 Victor Nava, "George Clooney fretted to White House that wife Amal could face sanctions over ICC case against Israel: report," New York Post, June 6, 2024, https://nypost.com/2024/06/06/us-news/george-clooney-fretted-to-white-house-that-wife-amal-could-face-sanctions-over-icc-case-against-israel-report/.

53 Joe Barnes, "Biden to skip Zelensky's peace summit for George Clooney fundraiser," The Telegraph, June 4, 2024, https://www.telegraph.co.uk/us/politics/2024/06/04/biden-to-skip-zelenskys-peace-summit-for-clooney-fundraiser/.

54 Agence France Presse, "Netanyahu Says 'Disappointed' Biden Won't Support ICC Sanctions," Barron's, June 2, 2024, https://www.barrons.com/news/netanyahu-says-disappointed-biden-won-t-support-icc-sanctions-72666813.

55 Darlene Superville and Will Weissert, "Clooney and Roberts help Biden raise $30 million-plus at a star-studded Hollywood gala," Associated Press, June 16, 2024, https://apnews.com/article/biden-hollywood-fundraiser-clooney-roberts-ukraine-summit-40081471c93faa68de5c4aa30455303b.

56 George Clooney, "I Love Joe Biden. But We Need a New Nominee," The New York Times, July 10, 2024, https://www.nytimes.com/2024/07/10/opinion/joe-biden-democratic-nominee.html.

57 Avril Haines, "Statement from Director of National Intelligence Avril Haines on Recent Iranian Influence Efforts," Office of the Director of National Intelligence, https://www.dni.gov/index.php/newsroom/press-releases/press-releases-2024/3842-statement-from-director-of-national-intelligence-avril-haines-on-recent-iranian-influence-efforts.

58 Summer Said, Benoit Faucon, and Stephen Kalin, "Iran Helped Plot Attack on Israel Over Several Weeks," *The Wall Street Journal*, October 8, 2023, https://www.wsj.com/world/middle-east/iran-israel-hamas-strike-planning-bbe07b25.

59 Haley Britzky, Natasha Bertrand, and Oren Liebermann, "Three US troops killed in drone attack in Jordan, more than 30 injured," CNN, https://www.cnn.com/2024/01/28/politics/us-troops-drone-attack-jordan/index.html.

60 M. J. Lee, Kevin Liptak, and Priscilla Alvarez, "Biden tells Netanyahu US will not participate in any counter-strike against Iran," CNN, https://www.cnn.com/2024/04/14/politics/biden-netanyahu-israel-iran-response/index.html.

61 Simon Lewis and Humeyra Pamuk, "State Dept says US actively pursuing the creation of a Palestinian state," Reuters, January 31, 2024, https://www.reuters.com/world/state-dept-says-us-actively-pursuing-creation-palestinian-state-2024-01-31/.

62 Summer Said and Rory Jones, "Gaza Chief's Brutal Calculation: Civilian Bloodshed Will Help Hamas," *The Wall Street Journal*, June 10, 2024, https://www.wsj.com/world/middle-east/gaza-chiefs-brutal-calculation-civilian-bloodshed-will-help-hamas-626720e7.

Chapter Two

1 Victoria C. Gardner Coates, *David's Sling: A History of Democracy in Ten Works of Art* (New York: Encounter Books, 2016), 240–42.

2 Émile Zola, "J'Accuse . . . !," *L'Aurore*, January 13, 1898.

3 Philip Ball, "How 2 Pro-Nazi Nobelists Attacked Einstein's 'Jewish Science,'" *Scientific American*, February 13, 2015, https://www.scientificamerican.com/article/how-2-pro-nazi-nobelists-attacked-einstein-s-jewish-science-excerpt1/.

4 Andrew Robinson, *Einstein on the Run: How Britain Saved the World's Greatest Scientist* (New Haven: Yale University Press, 2018).

5 Lewi Stone, "Quantifying the Holocaust: Hyperintense kill rates during the Nazi genocide," *Science Advances* 5 (1) (January 2019), https://www.science.org/doi/10.1126/sciadv.aau7292.

6 Rossella Tercatin, "Albert Einstein's letter denouncing antisemitism in US academia on sale," *The Jerusalem Post*, August 27, 2019, https://www.jpost.com/diaspora/albert-einsteins-letter-denouncing-antisemitism-in-us-academia-on-sale-599830.

7   Barry Strauss, "Jewish Roots in the Land of Israel/Palestine," Hoover Institution, February 6, 2024, https://www.hoover.org/research/jewish-roots-land-israelpalestine.

8   Isaiah 42:1–3.

9   Herodotus, *The Histories*, IV.39.

10   Daniel Avelar and Bianca Ferrari, "Israel and Palestine: a story of modern colonialism," openDemocracy, May 29, 2018, https://www.opendemocracy.net/en/north-africa-west-asia/israel-and-palestine-story-of-modern-colonialism/.

11   Johanna Regev et al, Radiocarbon chronology of Iron Age Jerusalem reveals calibration offsets and architectural developments," *PNAS* 121 (19) (April 2024), https://www.pnas.org/doi/10.1073/pnas.2321024121.

12   "The British Army in Palestine," National Army Museum, https://www.nam.ac.uk/explore/conflict-Palestine (accessed September 4, 2024).

13   "Jewish Legion (1915–1918)," Jewish Virtual Library, https://www.jewishvirtuallibrary.org/jewish-legion (accessed September 4, 2024).

14   Victoria Coates, "Peace Won't Come Until Palestinians Accept 'Plan A' Doesn't Exist," *The Daily Signal*, October 22, 2023, https://www.dailysignal.com/2023/10/22/peace-wont-come-until-palestinians-accept-plan-a-doesnt-exist/.

15   Ambassador Richard Holbrooke, "President Truman's Decision to Recognize Israel," *Jerusalem Center for Security and Foreign Affairs* 563 (May 2008), https://jcpa.org/article/president-truman%E2%80%99s-decision-to-recognize-israel/.

16   Michael David Sklaroff and Dr. Robert B. Sklaroff, "Judaism's Unique Impact On America's Constitution," *The Jewish Press*, December 31, 2008, https://www.jewishpress.com/indepth/opinions/judaisms-unique-impact-on-americas-constitution/2008/12/31/.

17   Richard Brookhiser, "Did George Washington really love the Jews?," *Forward*, February 21, 2022 (originally published 2017), https://forward.com/opinion/360674/did-george-washington-really-love-the-jews/.

18   George Washington, "From George Washington to the Hebrew Congregation in Newport, Rhode Island," August 18, 1790," Founders Online, National Archives, https://founders.archives.gov/documents/Washington/05-06-02-0135. Original source: *The Papers of George Washington, Presidential Series, vol. 6, 1 July 1790–30 November 1790*, ed. Mark A. Mastromarino (Charlottesville: University Press of Virginia, 1996), 284–286.

19 John Adams, "From John Adams to Mordecai M. Noah," March 15, 1819, Founders Online, National Archives, https://founders.archives.gov/documents/Adams/99-02-02-7097.

20 Abraham Lincoln, "Address to the New Jersey State Senate," Abraham Lincoln Online, February 21, 1861.

21 Norman Podhoretz, "J'Accuse," *Commentary*, September 1982, https://www.commentary.org/articles/norman-podhoretz/jaccuse/.

22 M. J. C. Warren, "Why 'Judeo-Christian values' are a dog-whistle myth peddled by the far right," *The Conversation*, November 7, 2017, https://theconversation.com/why-judeo-christian-values-are-a-dog-whistle-myth-peddled-by-the-far-right-85922; James Loeffler, "The Problem With the 'Judeo-Christian Tradition,'" *The Atlantic*, August 1, 2020, https://www.theatlantic.com/ideas/archive/2020/08/the-judeo-christian-tradition-is-over/614812/.

23 Dan Falk, "One Hundred Years Ago, Einstein Was Given a Hero's Welcome by America's Jews," *Smithsonian Magazine*, April 2, 2021, https://www.smithsonianmag.com/history/one-hundred-years-ago-einstein-was-given-heros-welcome-americas-jews-180977386/.

24 Holbrooke, "President Truman's Decision to Recognize Israel."

25 "The Sinai-Suez Campaign: President Eisenhower & PM Ben-Gurion on Israeli Withdrawal from Sinai (November 7–8, 1956)," Jewish Virtual Library, https://www.jewishvirtuallibrary.org/president-eisenhower-and-pm-ben-gurion-on-israeli-withdrawal-from-sinai-november-1956 (accessed September 4, 2024).

26 Mitch Ginsburg, "When Moshe Dayan delivered the defining speech of Zionism," *The Times of Israel*, April 28, 2016, https://www.timesofisrael.com/when-moshe-dayan-delivered-the-defining-speech-of-zionism/.

27 Tom Segev, *A State At Any Cost: The Life of David Ben-Gurion*, trans. Haim Watzman (New York: Farrar, Straus and Giroux, 2019), 405.

28 "The 1967 Arab-Israeli War," Department of State Office of the Historian, https://history.state.gov/milestones/1961-1968/arab-israeli-war-1967 (accessed September 4, 2024).

29 United Nations Security Council, "Resolution 242," November 22, 1967, http://unscr.com/en/resolutions/doc/242.

30 Joel Achenbach, "Did the news media, led by Walter Cronkite, lose the war in Vietnam?," *The Washington Post*, May 25, 2018, https://www.washingtonpost. com/national/did-the-news-media-led-by-walter-cronkite-lose-the-war-in-vietnam/2018/05/25/a5b3e098-495e-11e8-827e-190efaf1f1ee_story.html.

31 Lynn Elber, "Jane Fonda says she regrets her 'horrible' Vietnam War protest on a North Vietnamese anti-aircraft gun," Associated Press via *Business Insider*, July 30, 2018, https://www.businessinsider.com/jane-fonda-says-she-regrets-her-horrible-vietnam-war-protest-2018-7.

32 "How Richard Nixon Saved Israel," Richard Nixon Foundation, October 8, 2010, https://www.nixonfoundation.org/2010/10/how-richard-nixon-saved-israel/.

33 David Stout, "Israel's Nuclear Arsenal Vexed Nixon," *The New York Times*, November 29, 2007, https://www.nytimes.com/2007/11/29/world/middleeast/29nixon.html.

34 Congressional Research Service, "U.S. Foreign Aid to Israel," RL33222, March 1, 2023, https://crsreports.congress.gov/product/pdf/RL/RL33222.

35 "Camp David Accords and the Arab-Israeli Peace Process," Department of State Office of the Historian, https://history.state.gov/milestones/1977-1980/camp-david.

36 United Nations, "Treaty No. 17813: Egypt and Israel, March 26, 1979," United Nations Treaty Series 1979, https://treaties.un.org/doc/publication/unts/volume%20 1136/volume-1136-i-17813-english.pdf.

37 Saundra Saperstein and Sandra R. Gregg, "Reagan Pledges U.S., Israel Will 'Stand Together,'" *The Washington Post*, December 4, 1983, https://www.washingtonpost. com/archive/politics/1983/12/05/reagan-pledges-us-israel-will-stand-together/ bfde4ca9-33d6-41a6-adc4-0576a3f8031c/.

38 Congressional Research Service, "U.S. Foreign Aid to Israel."

39 Arnon Gutfeld, "The 1981 AWACS Deal: AIPAC and Israel Challenge Reagan," The Begin-Sadat Center for Strategic Studies, November 8, 2018, https://besacenter. org/reagan-saudi-awacs-aipac/.

40 "U.S.-Israel Formal Agreements: Memorandum of Understanding on Strategic Cooperation (November 30, 1981)," Jewish Virtual Library, https://www.jewishvirtuallibrary.org/u-s-israel-memorandum-of-understanding-on-strategic-cooperation-november-1981 (accessed September 4, 2024).

41 United Nations, "United States of America and Israel: Exchange of notes constituting an agreement concerning general security of military information. Tel Aviv, 30 July 1982 and Jerusalem, 10 December 1982," United Nations Treaty Series 1998, https://www.jewishvirtuallibrary.org/jsource/US-Israel/securityofinfo.pdf; Daniel Henninger, "Ronald Reagan Just Saved Israel From Iran's Attack," *The Wall Street Journal*, April 17, 2024, https://www.wsj.com/articles/ronald-reagan-just-saved-israel-iran-missile-defense-7c6847d1.

42 President Ronald Reagan, "Address to the Nation on Defense and National Security," via Ronald Reagan Presidential Library and Museum, March 23, 1983, https://www.reaganlibrary.gov/archives/speech/address-nation-defense-and-national-security.

43 "Nuclear Arms Race," C-SPAN, September 10, 1986, https://www.c-span.org/video/?150439-1/nuclear-arms-race.

44 "Striking a Bullet with a Bullet: HOE," Lockheed Martin, October 1, 2020, https://www.lockheedmartin.com/en-us/news/features/history/hoe.html.

45 "IMDO- Israel Missile Defense Organization: Innovative Strength," Israel Ministry of Defense, https://english.mod.gov.il/About/Innovative_Strength/Pages/IMDO_Israel_Missile_Defense_Organization.aspx (accessed September 4, 2024).

46 Hanan Shai, "The 1982 Lebanon War and Its Repercussions for Israel's National Security," The Begin-Sadat Center for Strategic Studies, BESA Center Perspectives Paper No. 1,596, June 4, 2020, https://besacenter.org/1982-lebanon-repercussions/.

47 Rumsfeld, *Known and Unknown*, 9–10.

48 "Rocket & Mortar Attacks Against Israel by Date (2001–Present)," Jewish Virtual Library, https://www.jewishvirtuallibrary.org/palestinian-rocket-and-mortar-attacks-against-israel (accessed September 4, 2024).

49 Shlomo Maital, "Iron Dome: The inside story," *The Jerusalem Post*, July 15, 2021, https://www.jpost.com/jerusalem-report/iron-dome-the-inside-story-673995. I also met with Levin at Rafael in 2014 and heard this story firsthand.

50 Robert Johnson, "Israeli Wedding Video Shows Missile Defense Taking Out Rockets," *Business Insider*, November 16, 2012, https://www.businessinsider.com/guests-in-this-wedding-video-watch-israels-missile-defense-system-save-the-day-2012-11.

51 Congressional Research Service, "U.S. Foreign Aid to Israel."

52 Seth J. Frantzman, "Israel and US begin Arrow-4 development," *DefenseNews*, February 18, 2021, https://www.defensenews.com/industry/techwatch/2021/02/18/israel-and-us-begin-arrow-4-development/.

53 Ben Sales, "What is the Iron Dome? All about the missile defense system that changed how Israelis experience war," Jewish Telegraphic Agency, May 14, 2021, https://www.jta.org/2021/05/14/israel/what-is-the-iron-dome-all-about-the-missile-defense-system-that-changed-how-israelis-experience-war.

54 Ron Kampeas, "Biden administration supports replenishing Iron Dome after Gaza conflict," Jewish Telegraphic Agency, June 3, 2021, https://www.jta.org/2021/06/03/politics/biden-administration-supports-replenishing-iron-dome-after-gaza-conflict.

55 Kyle Mizokami, "Israel's Uzi Submachine Gun: The Story of an Iconic Weapon," *The National Interest*, September 9, 2020, https://nationalinterest.org/blog/reboot/israels-uzi-submachine-gun-story-iconic-weapon-168589.

56 "Fact Sheet U.S.–Israel Economic Relationship," U.S. Embassy in Israel, https://il.usembassy.gov/our-relationship/policy-history/fact-sheet-u-s-israel-economic-relationship/ (accessed September 5, 2024).

57 Joseph Morgenstern, "Apple's history and development in Israel," *The Jerusalem Post*, February 26, 2015, https://www.jpost.com/Business/Apples-history-and-development-in-Israel-392387.

58 Abigail Klein Leichman, "6 Top Tomato Innovations from Israeli Experts," *Israel21c*, November 1, 2018, https://www.israel21c.org/6-top-tomato-innovations-from-israeli-experts/.

59 Julie Bort, "Waze cofounder tells us how his company's $1 billion sale to Google really went down," *Business Insider*, August 13, 2015, https://www.businessinsider.com/how-google-bought-waze-the-inside-story-2015-8.

60 "Most Influential Countries," *U.S. News & World Report*, https://www.usnews.com/news/best-countries/most-influential-countries (accessed September 5, 2024).

61 Hilary Faverman, "Innovation Diplomacy: Bringing Israel's Start-Up Nation Story to the World," *The Times of Israel*, June 2, 2023, https://www.timesofisrael.com/spotlight/the-key-to-peace-is-innovation-diplomacy/.

62 "How A Quest To Save Soviet Jews Changed The World," *All Things Considered*, NPR, October 30, 2010, https://www.npr.org/2010/10/30/130936993/how-a-quest-to-save-soviet-jews-changed-the-world.

63 Stuart Winer and TOI Staff, "Israel and Russia dedicate Jerusalem memorial to WWII Leningrad siege," *The Times of Israel*, January 23, 2020, https://www.timesofisrael.com/israel-russia-dedicate-jerusalem-memorial-to-wwii-leningrad-siege/.

64 Roi Feder, "What China's New Silk Road Means for Israel," *Diplomatic Courier*, September 1, 2016, https://www.diplomaticcourier.com/posts/chinas-new-silk-road-means-israel.

65 "China: Value of investment from China in Israel from 2010 to 2021," Statista, https://www.statista.com/statistics/1384126/china-investment-in-israel/#:~:text=In%202021%2C%20China%20invested%20over%202%20billion%20U.S.,worth%20around%201.4%20billion%20U.S.%20dollars%20in%202010.

66 Michael Wilner, "U.S. Navy may stop docking in Haifa after Chinese take over port," *The Jerusalem Post*, December 15, 2018, updated December 16, 2018, https://www.jpost.com/Israel-News/US-Navy-may-stop-docking-in-Haifa-after-Chinese-take-over-port-574414.

67 TOI Staff, "Chinese company connects Tel Aviv rail, Tehran," *The Times of Israel*, July 6, 2015, https://www.timesofisrael.com/chinese-company-connects-tel-aviv-rail-tehran/#:~:text=The%20Chinese%20company%20digging%20the%20tunnels%20for%20Tel,to%20help%20build%20Tel%20Aviv%E2%80%99s%20long-awaited%20light%20rail.

68 Simone Lipkind, Fickle Friends: Sino-Israeli Ties Buckle Amid War With Hamas," *Asia Unbound*, January 25, 2024, https://www.cfr.org/blog/fickle-friends-sino-israeli-ties-buckle-amid-war-hamas.

Chapter Three

1 David B. Ottaway and John M. Goshko, "U.S., In Effect, Recognizes the PLO," *The Washington Post*, December 16, 1988, https://www.washingtonpost.com/archive/politics/1988/12/16/us-in-effect-recognizes-the-plo/fd3ed3ef-1082-4d1e-8e51-45d84acf53be/.

2 Robert Pear, "Shultz's 'No' to Arafat; Personal Disgust for Terrorism Is at Root Of Secretary's Decision to Rebuff the P.L.O.," *The New York Times*, November 28, 1988, https://www.nytimes.com/1988/11/28/world/shultz-s-no-arafat-personal-disgust-for-terrorism-root-secretary-s-decision.html.

3 Youssef M. Ibrahim, "War in the Gulf: The P.L.O.; Arafat, the Survivor, Now Finds Support Vanishing," *The New York Times*, February 13, 1991, https://www.nytimes.com/1991/02/13/world/war-in-the-gulf-the-plo-arafat-the-survivor-now-finds-support-vanishing.html.

4   "After the War: The President; Transcript of President Bush's Address on End of the Gulf War," *The New York Times*, March 7, 1991, https://www.nytimes. com/1991/03/07/us/after-war-president-transcript-president-bush-s-address-end-gulf-war.html.

5   Yitzhak Rabin, "Israeli Chief of Staff Yitzhak Rabin: The Right of Israel," Center for Israel Education, June 28, 1967, https://israeled.org/wp-content/uploads/2017/02/1967.6.28-Rabin-The-Right-of-Israel.pdf.

6   Meron Medzini, "Rabin and Hussein: From Enemies at War to Partners in Peace," in P. R. Kumaraswamy, ed., *The Palgrave Handbook of the Hashemite Kingdom of Jordan* (Singapore: Palgrave Macmillan Singapore, 2019): 435–46.

7   Clyde Haberman, "The Jordan–Israel Accord: The Overview; Israel and Jordan Sign a Peace Accord," *The New York Times*, October 27, 1994, https://www.nytimes. com/1994/10/27/world/the-jordan-israel-accord-the-overview-israel-and-jordan-sign-a-peace-accord.html.

8   Bruce Riedel, "5 years on, remembering the path to peace for Jordan and Israel," Brookings, October 23, 2019, https://www.brookings.edu/articles/25-years-on-remembering-the-path-to-peace-for-jordan-and-israel/.

9   Eric Pace, "The Black September Guerrillas: Elusive Trail in Seven Countries," *The New York Times*, October 12, 1972, https://www.nytimes.com/1972/10/12/archives/the-black-september-guerrillas-elusive-trail-in-seven-countries.html.

10 "Yasir Arafat's Timeline of Terror," CAMERA, November 13, 2004, https://www. camera.org/article/yasir-arafat-s-timeline-of-terror/.

11 Paul Hofmann, "Dramatic Session," *The New York Times*, November 14, 1974, https://www.nytimes.com/1974/11/14/archives/dramatic-session-plo-head-says-he-bears-olive-branch-and-guerrilla.html.

12 Raymond H. Anderson, "In a U.N. Corner. Lobby, Arafat Held Audiences," *The New York Times*, November 14, 1974, https://www.nytimes.com/1974/11/14/archives/in-a-un-corner-lobby-arafat-held-audiences-heads-of-missions.html.

13 Wikisource contributors, "Yasser Arafat's 1974 UN General Assembly speech," Wikisource, November 3, 1974, https://en.wikisource.org/w/index.php?title=Yasser_Arafat%27s_1974_UN_General_Assembly_speech&oldid=13033656 (accessed September 5, 2024).

14 Paul Hofmann, U.N. Votes 72–35, To Term Zionism Form of Racism," *The New York Times*, November 11, 1975, https://www.nytimes.com/1975/11/11/archives/un-votes-7235-to-term-zionism-form-of-racism-us-asserts-it-will.html.

15 "SNL Transcripts: Robert Klein: 11/15/75: Weekend Update with Chevy Chase,"
    SNL Transcripts Tonight, https://snltranscripts.jt.org/75/75eupdate.phtml.

16 "Yasir Arafat's Timeline of Terror," CAMERA.

17 Efraim Krsh, "Arafat's Grand Strategy," *Middle East Quarterly* (Spring 2004),
    https://www.academia.edu/11231443/Arafats_Grand_Strategy.

18 Bill Clinton, *My Life: The Presidential Years*, vol. 2 (New York: Vintage, 2005).

19 Bill Clinton, *My Life*.

20 Helene Cooper, "Look Who's Reboarding That Clintonian Shuttle," *The New York
    Times*, April 1, 2007, https://www.nytimes.com/2007/04/01/weekinreview/01coo-
    per.html.

21 Elliott Abrams, *Tested by Zion: The Bush Administration and the Israeli–Palestinian
    Conflict* (Cambridge: Cambridge University Press, 2013), 244–61.

22 Ed Pilkington, "US abstains as UN security council backs Israel-Gaza cease-
    fire resolution," *The Guardian*, January 8, 2009, https://www.theguardian.com/
    world/2009/jan/09/usforeignpolicy-unitednations.

23 Abrams, *Tested by Zion*, 296–303.

24 Saeed Dehghan and David Smith, "US had extensive contact with Ayatollah
    Khomeini before Iran revolution," *The Guardian*, June 10, 2016, https://www.
    theguardian.com/world/2016/jun/10/ayatollah-khomeini-jimmy-carter-adminis-
    tration-iran-revolution.

25 U.S. Congress, "Executive Summary of the Report of the Commission to Assess
    the Ballistic Missile Threat to the United States," July 15, 1998, via FAS Intelligence
    Resource Program, https://irp.fas.org/threat/bm-threat.htm.

26 Zareen Syed and Alysa Guffey, "Students at University of Chicago set up protest
    encampment in solidarity with Gaza as movement grows," *Chicago Tribune*, May 3,
    2024, https://www.chicagotribune.com/2024/04/29/university-of-chicago-gaza-en-
    campment/.

27 Lani Guinier and Gerald Torres, "Derrick Bell: the Scholar Remembered," *The
    Chronicle of Higher Education*, October 10, 2011, https://www.chronicle.com/arti-
    cle/derrick-bell-the-scholar-remembered/.

28 "Obama Speaks at Harvard Law in '90," *Frontline*, PBS, April 24, 1990, https://
    www.pbs.org/video/frontline-obama-speaks-at-harvard-law-in-90/.

29 Associated Press, "CIA publicly acknowledges 1953 coup it backed in Iran was undemocratic as it revisits 'Argo' rescue," NBC News, October 12, 2023, https://www.nbcnews.com/news/us-news/cia-publicly-acknowledges-1953-coup-backed-iran-was-undemocratic-revis-rcna120154.

30 Ray Takeyh, "The Coup Against Democracy That Wasn't," *Commentary*, December 2021, https://www.commentary.org/articles/ray-takeyh/iran-1953-coup-america/.

31 "'It's Always About Oil': CIA & MI6 Staged Coup in Iran 70 Years Ago, Destroying Democracy in Iran," DemocracyNow!, August 23, 2023, https://www.democracynow.org/2023/8/23/ervand_abrahamian_iran_coup_1953_anniversary.

32 President Barack Obama, "Remarks by the President at Cairo University, 6-04-09," June 4, 2009, https://obamawhitehouse.archives.gov/the-press-office/remarks-president-cairo-university-6-04-09.

33 Ian Black, Saeed Kamali Dehghan, and Haroon Siddique, "Iran elections: Mousavi lodges appeal against Ahmadinejad victory," *The Guardian*, June 14, 2009, https://www.theguardian.com/world/2009/jun/14/iran-election-mousavi-appeal.

34 "The 2009 Green Revolution (Iranian elections)," Alfred Yaghobzadeh Photography, 2009, https://www.alfredyaghobzadehphoto.com/-/galleries/gallery/iran/the-2009-green-revolution-iranian-elections/-/medias/5d96b3d9-2321-4a7c-a070-286902d4cb7c-the-2009-green-revolution-iranian-elections.

35 Richard Pendlebury, "The YouTube Martyr: How Neda Agha Soltan has become the symbol that could help topple Iran's fanatical rulers," *Daily Mail*, June 23, 2009, https://www.dailymail.co.uk/news/article-1195060/The-YouTube-Martyr-How-Neda-Agha-Soltan-symbol-help-topple-Irans-fanatical-rulers.html.

36 Helene Cooper and David E. Sanger, "Obama Condemns Iran's Iron Fist Against Protests," *The New York Times*, June 23, 2009, https://www.nytimes.com/2009/06/24/us/politics/24webobama.html.

37 John Kerry, "With Iran, Think Before You Speak," *The New York Times*, June 17, 2009, https://www.nytimes.com/2009/06/18/opinion/18kerry.html.

38 Dennis Ross, "The inside story of Obama's Iran strategy," *Politico*, October 8, 2015, https://www.politico.eu/article/the-inside-story-of-obamas-path-to-yes-on-iran-netanhayu-israel-iran/.

39 Peter Baker and Jodi Rudoren, "Obama and Netanyahu: A Story of Slights and Crossed Signals," *The New York Times*, November 8, 2015, https://www.nytimes.com/2015/11/09/us/politics/obama-and-netanyahu-a-story-of-slights-and-crossed-signals.html.

40 Vice President Joseph R. Biden, "Remarks by Vice President Biden: The Enduring Partnership Between the United States and Israel," March 11, 2010, https://obamawhitehouse.archives.gov/the-press-office/remarks-vice-president-biden-enduring-partnership-between-united-states-and-israel.

41 Robert Farley, "Operation Opera: How Israel Killed Saddam Hussein's Nuclear Bomb Dream," *The National Interest*, December 25, 2020, https://nationalinterest.org/blog/reboot/operation-opera-how-israel-killed-saddam-husseins-nuclear-bomb-dream-175218.

42 Isabel Kershner, "Ending Secrecy, Israel Says It Bombed Syrian Reactor in 2007," *The New York Times*, March 21, 2018, https://www.nytimes.com/2018/03/21/world/middleeast/israel-syria-nuclear-reactor.html.

43 "Two Men Charged in Alleged Plot to Assassinate Saudi Arabian Ambassador to the United States," Office of Public Affairs, U.S. Department of Justice, October 11, 2011, https://www.justice.gov/opa/pr/two-men-charged-alleged-plot-assassinate-saudi-arabian-ambassador-united-states.

44 Harriet Sherwood, "Obama calls on Israelis to be bold in seeking peace with Palestinians," *The Guardian*, March 21, 2013, https://www.theguardian.com/world/2013/mar/21/obama-strong-call-israel-palestinian-peace.

45 President Barack Obama, "Remarks of President Barack Obama To the People of Israel," March 21, 2013, https://obamawhitehouse.archives.gov/the-press-office/2013/03/21/remarks-president-barack-obama-people-israel.

46 Philip Gordon, "Remarks as Prepared by White House Coordinator for the Middle East, North Africa, and the Gulf Region Philip Gordon at the Ha'aretz Israel Conference for Peace," July 8, 2014, https://obamawhitehouse.archives.gov/the-press-office/2014/07/08/remarks-prepared-white-house-coordinator-middle-east-northafrica-and-gu.

47 Danielle Wiener-Bronner, "A Brief History of the Fraught Relationship Between Fatah and Hamas," *The Atlantic*, April 24, 2014, https://www.theatlantic.com/international/archive/2014/04/a-brief-history-of-the-fraught-relationship-between-fatah-and-hamas/361178/.

48 "Israel/Palestine: Killings of Three Abducted Youth," Human Rights Watch, July 1, 2014, https://www.hrw.org/news/2014/07/01/israel/palestine-killings-three-abducted-youth.

49 "Hamas Admits To Kidnapping And Killing Israeli Teens," NPR, August 22, 2014, https://www.npr.org/2014/08/22/342318367/hamas-finally-admits-to-kidnapping-and-killing-israeli-teens.

50   Sudarsan Raghavan, William Booth, and Griff White, "How a 72-hour truce in
     Gaza fell apart in less than 2 hours," *The Washington Post*, August 1, 2014, https://
     www.washingtonpost.com/world/israel-hamas-agree-to-72-hour-humanitarian-
     cease-fire/2014/08/01/059f1ff8-194e-11e4-9e3b-7f2f110c6265_story.html.

51   David Samuels, "The Aspiring Novelist Who Became Obama's Foreign-Policy
     Guru," *The New York Times*, May 5, 2016, https://www.nytimes.com/2016/05/08/
     magazine/the-aspiring-novelist-who-became-obamas-foreign-policy-guru.html.

52   Paul Lewis and Saeed Kamali Dehghan, "Obama: Iran nuclear deal debate is a
     choice between diplomacy and war," *The Guardian*, July 15, 2015, https://www.
     theguardian.com/us-news/2015/jul/15/obama-iran-nuclear-deal-diplomacy-war.

53   John B. Judis, "Ending the Israeli-Palestinian Conflict Is No Longer a Vital Amer-
     ican Interest," *The New Republic*, August 10, 2014, https://newrepublic.com/arti-
     cle/119022/2014-gaza-war-why-obama-and-kerry-have-failed-end-it.

54   Baker and Rudoren, "Obama and Netanyahu."

55   Ross, "The inside story of Obama's Iran strategy."

56   Jeffrey Goldberg, "The Crisis in U.S.-Israel Relations Is Officially Here," *The Atlan-
     tic*, October 28, 2014, https://www.theatlantic.com/international/archive/2014/10/
     the-crisis-in-us-israel-relations-is-officially-here/382031/.

57   Michael Wilner, "Obama gets lecture on peace talks from Netanyahu in White
     House meeting," *The Jerusalem Post*, March 3, 2014, https://www.jpost.com/Diplo-
     macy-and-Politics/WATCH-LIVE-Netanyahu-and-Obama-meet-at-the-White-
     House-344144.

58   Rodolfo Quevenco, "IAEA Board Adopts Landmark Resolution on Iran PMD
     Case," International Atomic Energy Agency, December 15, 2015, https://www.iaea.
     org/newscenter/news/iaea-board-adopts-landmark-resolution-on-iran-pmd-case.

59   Kian Sharifi, "Going Nuclear: Iran's New Rhetorical Deterrence," RadioFreeEurope,
     May 16, 2024, https://www.rferl.org/a/iran-nuclear-bomb-fatwa-doctrine/32949893.
     html. While frequently referenced, the fatwa itself has never been published.

60   United States Mission to the United Nations, "Treaty Obligations," https://usun.
     usmission.gov/mission/host-country-section/treaty-obligations/ (accessed Sep-
     tember 5, 2024), https://usun.usmission.gov/mission/host-country-section/trea-
     ty-obligations/.

61 Associated Press, "'A slap in the face': US officials 'extremely troubled' by Iran's next UN ambassador who took part in the Tehran hostage crisis," *Daily Mail*, April 2, 2014, https://www.dailymail.co.uk/news/article-2595434/US-troubled-Irans-choice-UN-ambassador.html.

62 Ed O'Keefe and Robert Costa, "Ted Cruz-sponsored bill to bar Iran's U.N. envoy from entering U.S. passes Senate," *The Washington Post*, April 7, 2014, https://www.washingtonpost.com/politics/ted-cruz-sponsored-bill-to-bar-irans-un-envoy-from-entering-us-passes-senate/2014/04/07/fceff50e-be8e-11e3-bcec-b71ee10e-9bc3_story.html.

63 "The Joint Comprehensive Plan of Action (JCPOA) at a Glance," Arms Control Association, March 2022, https://www.armscontrol.org/factsheets/joint-comprehensive-plan-action-jcpoa-glance.

64 "Press Availability on Nuclear Deal With Iran," U.S. Department of State, July 14, 2015, https://2009-2017.state.gov/secretary/remarks/2015/07/244885.htm.

65 "The Historic Deal that Will Prevent Iran from Acquiring a Nuclear Weapon," The White House, https://obamawhitehouse.archives.gov/issues/foreign-policy/iran-deal (accessed September 5, 2024).

66 Elise Labott, Nicole Gaouette, and Kevin Liptak, "US sent plane with $400 million in cash to Iran," CNN, August 4, 2016, https://www.cnn.com/2016/08/03/politics/us-sends-plane-iran-400-million-cash/index.html.

67 David Samuels, "The Aspiring Novelist Who Became Obama's Foreign-Policy Guru," *The New York Times*, May 5, 2016, https://www.nytimes.com/2016/05/08/magazine/the-aspiring-novelist-who-became-obamas-foreign-policy-guru.html.

68 Paul Lewis and Saeed Kamali Dehghan, "Obama: Iran nuclear deal debate is a choice between diplomacy and war," *The Guardian*, July 15, 2015, https://www.theguardian.com/us-news/2015/jul/15/obama-iran-nuclear-deal-diplomacy-war.

69 "Understanding the U.S. Compliance Certification and Why It Matters to the Iran Nuclear Deal," Arms Control Association, https://www.armscontrol.org/blog/2017-08-29/understanding-us-compliance-certification-why-matters-iran-nuclear-deal (accessed September 5, 2024).

70 David Remnick, "On and Off the Road with Barack Obama," *The New Yorker*, January 19, 2014, https://www.newyorker.com/magazine/2014/01/27/going-the-distance-david-remnick.

71   "President Obama Has Ended the War in Iraq," The White House, October 21, 2011, https://obamawhitehouse.archives.gov/blog/2011/10/21/president-obama-has-ended-war-iraq.

72   Priyanki Boghani, "Iraq's Shia Militias: The Double-Edged Sword Against ISIS," *Frontline*, PBS, March 21, 2017, https://www.pbs.org/wgbh/frontline/article/iraqs-shia-militias-the-double-edged-sword-against-isis/.

73   Anne Barnard, "Iran Gains Influence in Iraq as Shiite Forces Fight ISIS," *The New York Times*, March 5, 2015, https://www.nytimes.com/2015/03/06/world/middleeast/iran-gains-influence-in-iraq-as-shiite-forces-fight-isis.html.

Chapter Four

1   Jeremy Diamond, "Donald Trump tries to prove his Israel bona fides," CNN, March 21, 2016, https://www.cnn.com/2016/03/21/politics/hillary-clinton-aipac-speech-donald-trump/index.html.

2   Sarah Begley, "Read Donald Trump's Speech to AIPAC," *Time*, March 21, 2016, https://time.com/4267058/donald-trump-aipac-speech-transcript/.

3   David Weigel, "AIPAC's apology for Trump speech is unprecedented," *The Washington Post*, March 22, 2016, https://www.washingtonpost.com/news/post-politics/wp/2016/03/22/aipacs-apology-for-trump-speech-is-unprecedented/.

4   Jimmy Carter, "America Must Recognize Palestine," The Carter Center, November 28, 2016, https://www.cartercenter.org/news/editorials_speeches/jimmy-carter-nyt-112816.html.

5   JTA and TOI Staff, "US appeals court: Americans born in Jerusalem not from 'Israel,'" *The Times of Israel*, July 23, 2013, https://www.timesofisrael.com/us-appeals-court-rules-israel-to-stay-off-jerusalemite-passports/.

6   "First Jerusalem-born American gets U.S. passport that lists 'Israel' as birthplace," Reuters, October 30, 2020, https://www.reuters.com/article/world/first-jerusalem-born-american-gets-us-passport-that-lists-israel-as-birthpla-idUSKBN-27F28G/.

7   "S. 11 (115th): Jerusalem Embassy and Recognition Act," GovTrack, https://www.govtrack.us/congress/bills/115/s11/summary#oursummary (accessed September 5, 2024).

8   Ian Fisher, "Netanyahu Says U.S. Embassy 'Needs to Be' in Jerusalem," *The New York Times*, January 29, 2017, https://www.nytimes.com/2017/01/29/world/middleeast/benjamin-netanyahu-israel-jerusalem-embassy.html.

9   Ron Dermer, "Proud to Have Been an American," *The New York Sun*, March 17, 2005, https://www.nysun.com/article/opinion-proud-to-have-been-an-american.

10   Isabel Kershner, "Deadly Violence Erupts in Standoff Over Mosque in Jerusalem," *The New York Times*, July 21, 2017, https://www.nytimes.com/2017/07/21/world/middleeast/jerusalem-israel-protests-al-aqsa-mosque.html.

11   TOI Staff and Agencies, "US ambassador gives first glimpse of new embassy in Jerusalem," *The Times of Israel*, May 12, 2018, https://www.timesofisrael.com/us-ambassador-gives-first-glimpse-of-new-embassy-in-jerusalem/.

12   Aaron David Miller, "Recognizing Jerusalem as Israel's capital is a dangerous gambit," CNN, December 6, 2017, https://www.cnn.com/2017/12/03/opinions/jerusalem-capital-trump-opinion-miller/index.html.

13   "The long-term global consequences of Trump's Jerusalem move," *PBS News Hour*, PBS, December 12, 2017, https://www.pbs.org/newshour/show/the-long-term-global-consequences-of-trumps-jerusalem-move.

14   Letters, "Artists attack Trump over Jerusalem move," *The Guardian*, December 11, 2017, https://www.theguardian.com/world/2017/dec/11/artists-attack-trump-over-jerusalem-move.

15   Rebecca Kheel, "Overnight Defense: US opens Jerusalem embassy as violence erupts | Haspel committee vote set for Wednesday | Trump blasts White House leakers as 'traitors,'" *The Hill*, May 14, 2018, https://thehill.com/policy/defense/overnights/387652-overnight-defense-us-opens-jerusalem-embassy-as-violence-erupts-in/.

16   Editorial Board, "James Mattis: Toughness and Restraint at the Pentagon," *The New York Times*, January 12, 2017, https://www.nytimes.com/2017/01/12/opinion/james-mattis-toughness-and-restraint-at-the-pentagon.html.

17   Yeganeh Torbati, "Trump election puts Iran nuclear deal on shaky ground," Reuters, November 9, 2016, https://www.reuters.com/article/idUSKBN13427D/.

18   David E. Sanger and Ronen Bergman, "How Israel, in Dark of Night, Torched Its Way to Iran's Nuclear Secrets," *The New York Times*, July 5, 2018, https://www.nytimes.com/2018/07/15/us/politics/iran-israel-mossad-nuclear.html; David Albright, Olli Heinonen, and Andrea Stricker, "Summary of Report: The Plan: Iran's Nuclear Archive Shows It Planned to Build Five Nuclear Weapons by mid-2003," Institute for Science and International Security and Foundation for Defense of Democracies, https://isis-online.org/uploads/isis-reports/documents/Summary_The_Plan_for_Five_Nuclear_Weapons_Final.pdf#:~:text=The%20Nuclear%20Archive%20documents%20show%20that%20Iran%20planned,assessment%20of%20the%20International%20Atomic%20Energy%20Agency%20%28IAEA%29 (accessed September 5, 2024).

19   Albright, et al., "Summary of Report."

20   "Country Analysis Executive Summary: Iran," U.S. Energy Information Administration, last updated November 17, 2022, https://www.eia.gov/international/content/analysis/countries_long/Iran/pdf/iran_exe.pdf.

21   "Iran Sanctions under the Trump Administration," International Crisis Group, https://www.crisisgroup.org/middle-east-north-africa/gulf-and-arabian-peninsula/iran/iran-sanctions-under-trump-administration (accessed September 5, 2024).

22   President Donald J. Trump, "Statement from the President on the Designation of the Islamic Revolutionary Guard Corps as a Foreign Terrorist Organization," April 8, 2019, https://trumpwhitehouse.archives.gov/briefings-statements/statement-president-designation-islamic-revolutionary-guard-corps-foreign-terrorist-organization/.

23   Seyed Hossein Mousavian, "Commentary: Five reasons why Trump's Iran sanctions will fail," Reuters, November 1, 2018, https://www.reuters.com/article/opinion/commentary-five-reasons-why-trumps-iran-sanctions-will-fail-idUSKCN1N42QN/.

24   Suzanne Maloney, "What both Trump and his critics get wrong about the IRGC terrorist designation," Brookings, April 11, 2019, https://www.brookings.edu/articles/what-both-trump-and-his-critics-get-wrong-about-the-irgc-terrorist-designation/.

25   "Six charts that show how hard US sanctions have hit Iran," BBC, December 9, 2019, https://www.bbc.com/news/world-middle-east-48119109.

26   "Iran suffering 'severe distress' from US sanctions, says IMF," *Financial Times*, October 17, 2019, https://www.ft.com/middle-eastern-economy?mhq5j=e1&page=11.

27 Barbara Starr and Ryan Browne, "US suspects Iran is behind increasingly sophisticated rocket attacks on US bases in Iraq," CNN, December 9, 2019, https://www.cnn.com/2019/12/09/politics/us-iran-rocket-attacks/index.html.

28 Helen Regan, "How the Oman tanker attack played out," CNN, June 14, 2019, https://www.cnn.com/2019/06/14/middleeast/tanker-iran-us-timeline-intl-hnk/index.html.

29 Summer Said, Jared Malsin, and Jessica Donati, "U.S. Blames Iran for Attack on Saudi Oil Facilities," *The Wall Street Journal*, September 14, 2019, 43375.

30 Scott L. Montgomery, "Attacks on Saudi oil—why didn't prices go crazy?," *The Conversation*, September 23, 2019, https://theconversation.com/attacks-on-saudi-oil-why-didnt-prices-go-crazy-123823.

31 Mohseh Gains, Abigail Williams, and Saphora Smith, "Iraq rocket attack kills contractor, wounds U.S. service member," NBC News, February 15, 2021, https://www.nbcnews.com/news/world/iraq-rocket-attack-kills-contractor-wounds-u-s-service-member-n1257963.

32 Elena Moore and Roberta Rampton, "Timeline: How The U.S. Came To Strike And Kill A Top Iranian General," NPR, January 4, 2020, https://www.npr.org/2020/01/04/793364307/timeline-how-the-u-s-came-to-strike-and-kill-a-top-iranian-general.

33 Alice Friend, Mara Karlin, and Loren Dejonge Schulman, "Why did the Pentagon ever give Trump the option of killing Soleimani?," Brookings, January 14, 2020, https://www.brookings.edu/articles/why-did-the-pentagon-ever-give-trump-the-option-of-killing-soleimani/.

34 Peter Kenyon and Greg Myre, "A Look Back At What Happened After The Killing Of Iranian Gen. Qassem Soleimani," *All Things Considered*, NPR, January 1, 2021, https://www.npr.org/2021/01/01/952716680/a-look-back-at-what-happened-after-the-killing-of-iranian-gen-qassem-soleimani.

35 "Trump releases long-awaited Middle-East peace plan," BBC, January 28, 2020, https://www.bbc.com/news/world-middle-east-51288218.

36 David M. Halbfinger, "In Bahrain, U.S. Tries to Promote Mideast Peace Through Prosperity," *The New York Times*, June 25, 2019, https://www.nytimes.com/2019/06/25/world/middleeast/israel-palestinian-peace-kushner.html.

37 "Trump Middle East plan: Palestinians reject 'conspiracy,'" BBC, January 29, 2020, https://www.bbc.com/news/world-middle-east-51292865.

38 Warren P. Strobel and Dion Nissenbaum, "U.S. Arranges Secret Talks Between Israel, U.A.E. Over Iran," *The Wall Street Journal*, August 15, 2019, https://www.wsj.com/articles/u-s-arranges-secret-talks-between-israel-u-a-e-over-iran-11565870404.

39 Barak Ravid, "Scoop: U.S. pushing Arab states on non-belligerence pacts with Israel," *Axios*, December 3, 2019, https://www.axios.com/2019/12/03/us-israel-arab-states-non-belligerance-agreements.

40 Dion Nissenbaum, "A Secret U.S. Rescue in Yemen Played a Role in Mideast Peace Deal," *The Wall Street Journal*, October 19, 2020, https://www.wsj.com/articles/a-secret-u-s-rescue-in-yemen-played-a-role-in-mideast-peace-deal-11603099801.

41 "The UAE and the F-35: Frontline Defense for the UAE, US and Partners," Embassy of the United Arab Emirates, Washington DC, May 2021, https://www.uae-embassy.org/sites/default/files/2021-11/f-35_white_paper.pdf.

42 "United States Recognizes Morocco's Sovereignty Over Western Sahara," *American Journal of International Law* 115, no. 2 (2021): 318–23, https://doi.org/10.1017/ajil.2021.11.

43 Karim Mezran and Alissa Pavia, "Morocco and Israel are friendlier than ever thanks to the Abraham Accords. But what does this mean for the rest of North Africa?," Atlantic Council, October 7, 2021, https://www.atlanticcouncil.org/blogs/menasource/morocco-and-israel-are-friendlier-than-ever-thanks-to-the-abraham-accords-but-what-does-this-mean-for-the-rest-of-north-africa/.

44 Michael Wilner and Herb Keinon, "Kerry: 'The settler agenda is defining the future of Israel,'" *The Jerusalem Post*, December 28, 2016, https://www.jpost.com/arab-israeli-conflict/kerry-the-settler-agenda-is-defining-the-future-of-israel-476780.

45 "U.S. gives Palestinians $15 million for COVID-19 response: statement," Reuters, March 25, 2021, https://www.reuters.com/article/us-health-coronavirus-usa-palestianians-idUSKBN2BH3IW/.

46 Matt Spetalnick and Stephen Farrell, "U.S. restores assistance for Palestinians, to provide $235 million in aid," Reuters, April 7, 2021, https://www.reuters.com/article/us-palestinians-usa-blinken-idUSKBN2BU2XT/.

47 Jenny Leonard and Justin Sink, "Biden Plans $316 Million in Palestinian Aid, Reviving US Ties," *Bloomberg*, July 14, 2022, https://www.bloomberg.com/news/articles/2022-07-15/biden-plans-316-million-in-palestinian-aid-reviving-us-ties.

48 Adam Kredo, "Biden Admin Raised Concerns Palestinian Aid Would Boost Hamas. It Went Ahead With Aid Anyway," *The Washington Free Beacon*, August 16, 2023, https://freebeacon.com/biden-administration/biden-admin-raised-concerns-palestinian-aid-would-boost-hamas-it-went-ahead-with-aid-anyway/.

49 C. Todd Lopez, "Supplemental Bill Becomes Law, Provides Billions in Aid for Ukraine, Israel, Taiwan," *DOD News*, U.S. Department of Defense, April 24, 2024, https://www.defense.gov/News/News-Stories/Article/Article/3754718/supplemental-bill-becomes-law-provides-billions-in-aid-for-ukraine-israel-taiwan/#:~:text=The%20supplemental%20security%20bill%2C%20Biden%20said%2C%20helps%20Israel,populations%20caught%20in%20conflict%20zones%20across%20the%20globe.

50 Antony J. Blinken, Secretary of State, "Revocation of the Terrorist Designations of Ansarallah: Press Statement," U.S. Department of State, February 12, 2021, https://www.state.gov/revocation-of-the-terrorist-designations-of-ansarallah/.

51 Victoria Coates, "As Ukraine burns, Russia is manipulating Biden into accepting a weak new Iran nuclear deal. But haven't we learned that appeasement doesn't work, asks former deputy National Security Advisor Victoria Coates," *Daily Mail*, March 4, 2022, https://www.dailymail.co.uk/news/article-10578541/RUSSIA-manipulating-Biden-accepting-weak-new-Iran-nuclear-deal-VICTORIA-COATES.html.

52 Reuters, "Iranian oil exports end 2022 at a high, despite no nuclear deal," CNBC, January 15, 2023, https://www.cnbc.com/2023/01/15/iranian-oil-exports-end-2022-at-a-high-despite-no-nuclear-deal.html.

53 Ben Hubbard, "Iran's Allies Feel the Pain of American Sanctions," *The New York Times*, March 28, 2019, https://www.nytimes.com/2019/03/28/world/middleeast/iran-sanctions-arab-allies.html.

54 Bozorgmehr Sharafedin, "Inside Tehran's Soft War: How Iran Gained Influence In US Policy Centers," *Iran International*, https://content.iranintl.com/en/investigates/inside-tehran-softwar/ (accessed September 5, 2024).

55 Kylie Atwood, Alex Marquardt, Jeremy Herb and Zachary Cohen, "Biden's Iran envoy placed on leave after security clearance suspended amid investigation into possible mishandling of classified material, sources say," CNN, June 29, 2023, https://www.cnn.com/2023/06/29/politics/rob-malley-leave-investigation-classified-material/index.html.

56 Tom Durso, "Senior State Department Official to Join SPIA Faculty as Visiting Professor and Lecturer," Princeton School of Public and International Affairs, August 15, 2023, https://spia.princeton.edu/news/senior-state-department-official-join-spia-faculty-visiting-professor-and-lecturer.

57 Ranj Alaaldin, "The Popular Mobilization Force is turning Iraq into an Iranian client state," Brookings, February 2, 2024, https://www.brookings.edu/articles/the-popular-mobilization-force-is-turning-iraq-into-an-iranian-client-state/.

58 Dan De Luce, "Iranian-backed Houthi rebels in Yemen ramp up drone, missile attacks on Saudi Arabia," NBC News, March 12, 2021, https://www.nbcnews.com/news/world/iranian-backed-houthi-rebels-yemen-ramp-drone-missile-attacks-saudi-n1260488.

59 Aya Batrawy, "Drone attack in Abu Dhabi claimed by Yemen's rebels kills 3," Associated Press, January 17, 2022, https://apnews.com/article/business-dubai-united-arab-emirates-abu-dhabi-yemen-8bdefdf900ce46a6fd6c7bc685bf838a.

60 Michael Crowley, "U.S. to Return Houthis to Terrorism List," *The New York Times*, January 16, 2024, https://www.nytimes.com/2024/01/16/us/politics/houthis-terrorism-designation.html.

61 "Intel expert rips Biden's Hezbollah remark: 'What he said is ridiculous,'" Fox Business via YouTube, October 19, 2023, https://www.youtube.com/watch?v=30B-p1qZ2cY.

62 Mike Wagenheim, "'Accord'ing to State Department," *The Media Line*, June 11, 2021, https://themedialine.org/top-stories/according-to-the-state-department/.

63 Anna Foster, "Saudi Arabia: The significance of Biden's fist bump with crown prince," BBC, July 16, 2022, https://www.bbc.com/news/world-middle-east-62189543.

64 Mark Mazzetti, Ronen Bergman, Edward Wong, and Vivian Nereim, "Biden Administration Engages in Long-Shot Attempt for Saudi-Israel Deal," *The New York Times*, June 17, 2023, updated June 20, 2023, https://www.nytimes.com/2023/06/17/us/politics/biden-saudi-arabia-israel-palestine-nuclear.html.

65 Joel Gehrke, "State Department clarifies Biden comments on Israel-Saudi Arabia talks," *Washington Examiner*, July 16, 2024, https://www.washingtonexaminer.com/policy/foreign-policy/3085887/state-department-clarifies-biden-comments-on-israel-saudi-arabia-talks/.

66 TOI Staff, "Report: Netanyahu decides not to seek normalization with Saudis before US election," *The Times of Israel*, August 4, 2024, https://www.timesofisrael.com/report-netanyahu-decides-not-to-seek-normalization-with-saudis-before-us-election/.

67   Ben Rhodes, "A Foreign Policy for the World as It Is: Biden and the Search for a New American Strategy," *Foreign Affairs*, June 18, 2024, https://www.foreignaffairs.com/united-states/biden-foreign-policy-world-rhodes.

68   The Editorial Board, "Palestinian 'Pay for Slay' Keeps Growing," *The Wall Street Journal*, January 15, 2024, https://www.wsj.com/articles/palestinian-pay-for-slay-hamas-oct-7-israel-gaza-antony-blinken-ramallah-2dce9a22.

69   Jeremy Diamond, "Israel releases names and details of alleged involvement of UN-RWA employees in October 7 attacks," CNN, February 16, 2024, https://www.cnn.com/2024/02/16/middleeast/israel-allegations-unrwa-october-7-intl/index.html.

70   United States Senate Committee on Appropriations, "Bill Summary: State, Foreign Operations, and Related Programs Fiscal Year 2024 Appropriations Bill," March 21, 2024, https://www.appropriations.senate.gov/news/majority/bill-summary-state-foreign-operations-and-related-programs-fiscal-year-2024-appropriations-bill-conference.

71   Ilan Ben Zion, "Trump Israel trip 1st presidential flight from Saudi Arabia," Associated Press, May 22, 2017, https://apnews.com/general-news-337240bff-bee4beo8ddcd9c87f71213b; Robert Greenway, "Transforming the Middle East: The Origins, Impact, and Evolution of the Abraham Accords," Hudson Institute, March 9, 2021, https://www.hudson.org/foreign-policy/transforming-the-middle-east-the-origins-impact-and-evolution-of-the-abraham-accords.

72   Congressional Research Service, "Cooperative Security in the Middle East: History and Prospects," April 8, 2019, https://crsreports.congress.gov/product/pdf/IF/IF11173/2.

73   Robert Greenway, "Greater than the Sum of Its Parts: Abraham Accords Free Trade Area," Hudson Institute, February 28, 2023, https://www.hudson.org/foreign-policy/greater-sum-its-parts-abraham-accords-free-trade-area.

74   Andrea Stricker, "What to Know About Iran's Nuclear Program: Advanced Centrifuges," Foundation for Defense of Democracies, May 1, 2024, https://www.fdd.org/analysis/2024/05/01/what-to-know-about-irans-nuclear-program-advanced-centrifuges/.

75   Agence France Presse, "Iran Can Produce Fissile Material For Bomb In 'One Or Two Weeks': Blinken," *Barron's*, July 19, 2024, https://www.barrons.com/news/iran-capable-of-producing-fissile-material-in-one-or-two-weeks-blinken-f15c767c.

76 Robert Greenway, "Strength in Unity: A Sustainable US-Led Regional Security Construct in the Middle East," Hudson Institute, August 18, 2023, https://www.hudson.org/foreign-policy/strength-unity-sustainable-us-led-regional-security-construct-middle-east-robert-greenway.

77 Office of the Spokesperson, "Statement of the Co-Chairs of the First Middle East Strategic Alliance (MESA) Meeting of the Energy Pillar Working Group," U.S. Department of State, September 17, 2019, https://2017-2021.state.gov/statement-of-the-co-chairs-of-the-first-middle-east-strategic-alliance-mesa-meeting-of-the-energy-pillar-working-group/.

78 "U.S. energy facts explained," U.S. Energy Information Administration, last updated July 15, 2024, https://www.eia.gov/energyexplained/us-energy-facts/#:~:text=U.S.%20total%20annual%20energy%20production%20has%20exceeded%20total,of%20total%20U.S.%20primary%20energy%20production%20in%202023.

79 Fred Zeidman and Victoria Coates, "US and Israeli energy miracles can fuel the future—opinion," *The Jerusalem Post*, October 31, 2021, https://www.jpost.com/opinion/us-and-israeli-energy-miracles-can-fuel-the-future-opinion-683645.

80 Maayan Jaffe-Hoffman, "Israel reduced greenhouse gas emissions by 10% in 10 years—OECD," *The Jerusalem Post*, April 4, 2023, updated April 15, 2023, https://www.jpost.com/environment-and-climate-change/article-736381.

81 "Electricity 2024: Analysis and Forecast to 2026," IEA, January 2024, https://iea.blob.core.windows.net/assets/6b2fd954-2017-408e-bf08-952fdd62118a/Electricity2024-Analysisandforecastto2026.pdf.

82 Charles Ellinas, "Energy and geopolitics in the Eastern Mediterranean," Atlantic Council, February 16, 2024, https://www.atlanticcouncil.org/in-depth-research-reports/report/energy-and-geopolitics-in-the-eastern-mediterranean/.

83 David Wethe and Kevin Crowley, "Chevron to Buy Noble or $5 Billion in Rare Oil-Bust Deal," *Bloomberg*, July 20, 2020, https://www.bloomberg.com/news/articles/2020-07-20/chevron-agrees-to-buy-noble-energy-for-5-billion?leadSource=uverify%20wall.

84 Rory Jones and Jared Malsin, "Noble Energy, Israel's Delek to Supply Gas to Egypt in $15 Billion Deal," *The Wall Street Journal*, February 19, 2018, https://www.wsj.com/articles/noble-energy-israels-delek-to-supply-gas-to-egypt-in-15-billion-deal-1519070941.

85 "Who We Are," Chevron Israel, https://israel.chevron.com/en/about (accessed September 5, 2024).

86 Victoria Coates, "When Energy Markets And Geopolitics Collide," Hoover Institution, March 7, 2023, https://www.hoover.org/research/when-energy-markets-and-geopolitics-collide.

87 Ellie Cohanim, "The Time Has Come for a Domestic Anti-Semitism Czar in the U.S.," *Newsweek*, June 30, 2021, https://www.newsweek.com/time-has-come-domestic-anti-semitism-czar-us-opinion-1604886.

88 Kanishka Singh, "US anti-Muslim incidents hit record high in 2023 due to Israel-Gaza war," Reuters, April 2, 2024, https://www.reuters.com/world/us/us-anti-muslim-incidents-hit-record-high-2023-due-israel-gaza-war-2024-04-02/.

89 Jonathan A. Greenblatt, "The Growing Antisemitism Among Young Americans," Time, March 21, 2024, https://time.com/6958957/growing-antisemitism-young-americans/.

90 Mike Gonzalez and Mary Mobley, "How the Revolutionary Ecosystem Sustains Pro-Palestinian Protesters and the BLM Movement," The Heritage Foundation, June 25, 2024, https://www.heritage.org/global-politics/report/how-the-revolutionary-ecosystem-sustains-pro-palestinian-protesters-and-the.

91 Office of Public Affairs, "Federal Judge Hands Downs Sentences in Holy Land Foundation Case," U.S. Department of Justice, May 27, 2009, https://www.justice.gov/opa/pr/federal-judge-hands-downs-sentences-holy-land-foundation-case.

92 Jared Gans, "Vast majority of Americans back Israel over Hamas: Poll," *The Hill*, April 29, 2024, https://thehill.com/policy/international/4629597-americans-israel-hamas-gaza-student-protests-poll/.

93 Hussein Ibish, "The United States and Israel Are Coming Apart," *The Atlantic*, April 5, 2024, https://www.theatlantic.com/international/archive/2024/04/us-israel-rift-war-palestine/677972/.

94 Goldberg, "The Crisis in U.S.-Israel Relations Is Officially Here," *The Atlantic*, October 8, 2014, https://www.theatlantic.com/international/archive/2014/10/the-crisis-in-us-israel-relations-is-officially-here/382031/.